the DISTRICT
Short Break Guide

THE LAKE DISTRICT

HOW THE LAKES WERE FORMED

When viewed on a map, the lakes of Lakeland radiate outwards from a central, high plateau, in the shape of a starburst. This interesting landscape feature gives a clue to the complex geology of the region. Lakeland was not formed by a single process, but by several over many millennia. The oldest rocks, the smooth Skiddaw slates, are about 500 million years old, and were formed at the bottom of a shallow sea. A period of intense volcanic action followed, while earth movements below ground buckled the rocks of the Scafell range into its familiar jagged outline. About 300 million years ago, the area once again formed the bed of a shallow, coral-rich tropical sea. Then, around just 60 million years ago, more underground movement erupted the rocks into a huge dome, which fractured and split. The lakes and valleys themselves are the most recent features and were created about 15,000 years ago by glacier action during the last Ice Age. Further erosion since then has given us the familiar Lakeland scene we see today.

For the purposes of this guide, the Lake District is defined as being not only the central area of the National Park itself, but also much of Cumbria, to the east, and parts of Lancashire, to the south, so as to provide a more complete guide and holiday destination for visitors. The Lake District is one of the premier tourist spots of Britain and it can get busy in season at the main resorts, but it remains a largely unspoilt region, with many quiet backwaters. The mountains of Cumbria form the highest land in England and the area as a whole is one of the most scenically beautiful parts, not only of Britain, but of Europe.

THE NATIONAL PARK

The Lake District National Park was created in 1951 and is the largest in Britain, at some 866 sq miles (2,243 sq km). With a resident population of about 47,000, it excludes most towns of any size and stops short of the coastal region. It was created, following the National Parks Act of 1949, with the express intention of preserving the natural beauty of the region, whilst at the same time maintaining the way of life of the local community.

BORDER DISPUTES

Surprisingly, the land disputes between England and Scotland were not properly settled until the 18th century. Landowners on both sides of the border were constantly contesting their rights, and lightning raids to steal a crofter's stock or set fire to buildings were a common occurrence. Several towns, including Carlisle, Coldstream and, on the eastern coast, Berwick-on-Tweed, changed hands on more than one occasion. The last time the region was attacked by Scotland was during the Jacobite rising of 1745.

A BRIEF BACKGROUND TO THE REGION

LITERARY GREATS

It is not surprising that the magnificent landscapes of the Lake District have attracted their fair share of artists, photographers and, more especially perhaps, writers. Each, in their own way, has tried to capture the beauty of the scenery or used it as a source of inspiration for their work. Writers who have lived and worked here include such literary greats as Wordsworth and Coleridge, the celebrated Lakeland poets; Beatrix Potter, the much-loved children's author; and John Ruskin the author and art critic. In more recent times, the novelist Melvyn Bragg lives and has set many of his stories in the region, but the writer who, perhaps more than anyone, has captured the spirit of this timeless landscape is A. Wainwright, with his excellent series of guide books to the fells.

A MAJESTIC LANDSCAPE

The Lakeland landscape is one of the most richly beautiful and diverse in Europe, especially for such a comparatively small area. It is prettier and softer than the harsher mountain landscapes of Wales and Scotland and less bleak than the Pennines. Less grand, perhaps, than the major mountain chains of Europe, but majestic in the extreme. The great folds in the rocks were created during vast underground  movements in the Earth's turbulent past, when great mountain ranges were formed across the globe. The gentler aspects of the Lakeland scenery were created when the area formed a vast sea bed and the rocks were worn smooth by the action of water. The scene is an ever-changing one, and although the lakes were the last feature to appear, they are already silting up quite naturally. In 50,000 years time, they may no longer exist.

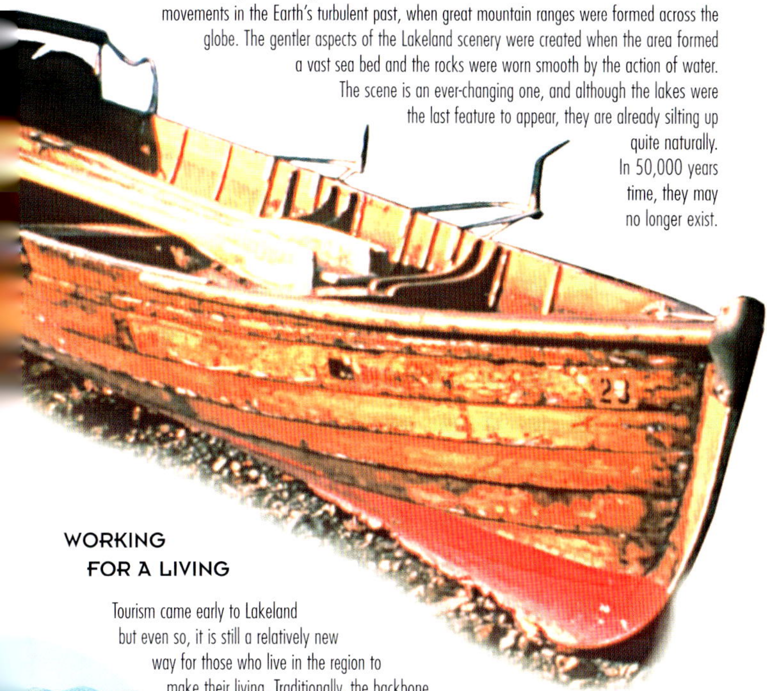

WORKING FOR A LIVING

Tourism came early to Lakeland but even so, it is still a relatively new way for those who live in the region to make their living. Traditionally, the backbone of the area was farming, as it still is, and there are many agricultural shows and gatherings where the two apparently opposed industries meet and rub shoulders. The area has also retained a great deal of its traditional ways and customs, which it has skilfully turned into visitor attractions (such as regional sports days, featuring local games and events), but without despoiling either its landscapes or its culture.

FAVOURITE BEACHES

The beaches of the northwest region are often overshadowed by the mountain scenery, but the area has some surprisingly lovely coastal resorts, with miles of fine sand. The northerly latitude can be a little bracing, but the beaches are often deserted and well worth the effort of discovering this little-appreciated aspect of Lakeland.

1 ALLONBY BAY

The small resort of Allonby was once popular with smugglers, but now finds favour with holiday-makers. In keeping with most other resorts along this section of coast, Allonby remains quite unspoilt and has not suffered at the hands of over commercialisation. There is a good beach of fine sand which is generally quite safe for bathing.

P WC |O| & - Aspatria

2 WHITEHAVEN

The port of Whitehaven owes its prosperity to the Lowthers, who developed what was a tiny fishing village in the 17th century into a major port. There are good sandy beaches at Whitehaven itself and miles of low dunes, with quiet beaches to the north. The beach at Whitehaven faces due west, into the Irish Sea, offering safe bathing and good water sports facilities. Its importance as a port has declined in recent years, but the town has developed instead into a popular holiday resort.

P WC |O| & - Whitehaven

3 ST. BEES

Surprisingly perhaps, when one considers that this region contains the highest ground in England, the coast of Cumbria is relatively flat. St. Bees Head contains the only sea cliffs on this stretch of coast. Footpaths lead from a car park to the headland. Fine, sandy beaches stretch for 17 miles (27 km) south of the headland. St. Bees village offers the usual seaside facilities. Bathing is generally safe, but be aware that tides can advance quickly.

P WC |O| & - St. Bees

4 SILLOTH

Silloth is the last holiday resort town of any size before reaching the Scottish border. It is a quaint town, with cobbled streets, that has grown up around its harbour. The sand and shingle beach offers good water sport facilities. At low tide patches of mud are exposed. It is best to avoid swimming when the tide is on the ebb because of undercurrents, but otherwise bathing is safe and the waters are very clean.

P WC ♿ 🚆 - Wigton

WARNING

The seas off the Cumbrian coast are not the friendliest in Britain, with many tricky currents where the Solway Firth meets the Irish Sea. There are special dangers in the Leven Estuary and Morecambe Bay, where shifting sea channels, fast-flowing tides and quick-sands make the area quite treacherous. Always stay within recognised safe-bathing areas and never attempt to cross wide areas of sand flats without the expert guidance of a Sand Pilot - 📞 01229 580935

5 GRANGE-OVER-SANDS

A charming resort, offering everything the modern holiday-maker desires. Tucked away from the westerly winds, where the River Kent meets Morecambe Bay, Grange-over-Sands enjoys a sheltered location. Although it has fine beaches, bathers are advised to beware the undercurrents, channels, quick sands and fast incoming tide. The beach itself, however, has fine sands and is ideal for sunbathing.

P WC ♿ 🚆 - Grange-over-Sands

6 MORECAMBE

Morecambe has developed into a resort of some renown by providing a range of attractions for visitors. There is a four-mile long promenade, offering parks, gardens, shops, cafés, amusement arcades and every conceivable form of holiday entertainment. The illuminations here are second only to Blackpool. The beaches at Morecambe are excellent (providing you keep clear of the danger areas at Morecambe Bay, further north), with fine sand. Bathing is good and there are excellent water sports facilities.

WC ♿ 🚆 - Morecambe

CHILDREN'S DAYS OUT

The following selection of places to visit has been specially chosen with children in mind, to provide that extra bit of excitement. They range from family days out at leisure complexes to wildlife parks and heritage centres which offer hands-on experiences to fuel lively imaginations and satisfy curiosity.

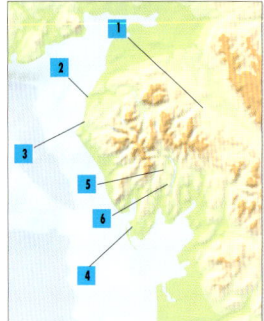

1 LOWTHER LEISURE PARK

Situated just off the A6 at Hackthorpe, near Penrith

The 150-acre Lowther Leisure Park has a selection of both open-air and under-cover rides in a peaceful, park setting, with fine walks for the more energetic.
Open daily, Apr.-Sept. 01931 712523

P WC ⚲ & 🚂 - Penrith

2 MARYPORT MARITIME MUSEUM

1 Senhouse Street

Maryport's fascinating maritime history is captured in this excellent museum, housed in an attractive building overlooking the harbour and alongside the Tourist Information Centre. The museum is especially good for children, with several displays geared towards meeting the requirements of the National Curriculum. Maryport is famous for two maritime personalities: Fletcher Christian, of 'Mutiny on the Bounty' fame and Thomas Henry Ismay, who founded the White Star Line, owners of the ill-fated 'Titanic'. Admission to the museum is free.
Open daily all year. 01900 813738

P nearby WC & limited 🚂 - Maryport

3 THE BEACON, WHITEHAVEN

West Strand

The story of Whitehaven's social, industrial and maritime heritage is vividly brought to life using comical characters, sounds, graphics, audio-visual presentations and interactive computer systems. One of the most interesting displays is the Weather Gallery, where you can monitor, forecast and even broadcast your own weather report using the same technology that television presenters use. Open all year, Tues.-Sun. and Bank Holiday Mon. 01946 592302

P WC ⚲ & 🚂 - Whitehaven

4 SOUTH LAKES WILD ANIMAL PARK

Crossgates, Dalton-in-Furness

This is the only zoological park in the Lake District and generally recognised as one of the leading conservation-minded zoos in Europe. The zoo covers 17 acres at Crossgates, near Dalton-in-

5 GRIZEDALE VISITOR CENTRE

Forest Enterprise, Grizedale, Hawkshead

Grizedale Forest is virtually an island between the vast expanses of Lake Windermere and Coniston Water, and their attendant river systems. It is the largest forest area in the Lake District and was one of the first Forestry Commission plantations to include a full range of visitor facilities and activities alongside its primary purpose of growing commercial timber.
The Visitor Centre offers an excellent introduction to the various aspects of forest management. There are numerous walks and picnic sites and an imaginative forest sculpture trail.
Open daily all year. ☎ 01229 860010

Furness, and is home to some of the rarest animal species on Earth. Co-ordinated breeding programmes ensure that many are saved from extinction in the wild. Special features at the park are the tiger conservation centre and walk-through Australian bush experience. Many of the animals wander freely around the park.
Open daily all year, except Christmas Day.
☎ 01229 466086

P WC 🍴 ♿ 🚂 - Dalton-in-Furness

P WC 🍴 ♿ 🚂 - Windermere

6 LAKESIDE AND HAVERTHWAITE RAILWAY

Haverthwaite Station, near Ulverston

The Lakeside and Haverthwaite Railway was once a branch line on the Furness Railway. It was an early attempt at catering for the tourist trade by connecting to steamer services on Lake Windermere. It is still possible to combine your trip with a cruise on one of the 'Windermere Lake Cruises' steamboats, disembarking at several places of interest around the lake, such as 'The World of Beatrix Potter' at Bowness (see page 8). Open Mar.-Nov. on advertised days.
☎ 015395 31594   P WC 🍴 ♿   🚂 - Ulverston

CHILDREN'S DAYS OUT

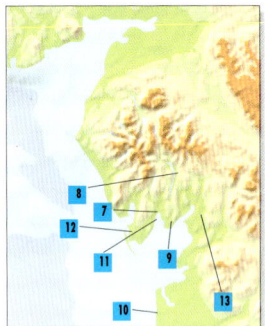

7 ABBOTS READING FARM
Haverthwaite, Ulverston

Abbots Reading Farm and Museum is a working Lakeland farm in the beautiful Rusland Valley, overlooking the Coniston Fells. The farm is an approved rare breeds centre. Enjoy native and rare breeds of farm animals, browse around the fascinating museum of bygone agricultural equipment, picnic in the orchard or simply let the kids enjoy the children's play area. There is no public transport direct to the farm, but Haverthwaite is served by the Lakeside and Haverthwaite Railway.

Open Wed.-Fri., May-Sept. 015395 31203 - Ulverston

8 THE WORLD OF BEATRIX POTTER

The Old Laundry, Crag Brow, Bowness-on-Windermere

No visit to the Lake District would be complete without a visit to the 'World of Beatrix Potter', situated at Bowness. The charming characters of the popular children's story books are brought lovingly to life in this exhibition, which features all the latest high-tech devices. It is located in the Old

9 LAKELAND MOTOR MUSEUM

In the grounds of Holker Hall, Cark-in-Cartmel

Have a look around this nostalgic collection of cars and motoring memorabilia. Other modes of transport are represented too, such as bygone bicycles, motor bikes and scooters. There is also a special exhibition relating to the Campbells, including the famous 'Bluebird'. Donald Campbell was tragically killed on Coniston Water in 1967 during an attempt to break the world water-speed record.

Open Sun.-Fri., Apr.-Oct.
015395 58509
 - Cark

Laundry, which also houses a small theatre and regularly holds special exhibitions and events.

Open daily all year, except Christmas and late Jan. 015394 88444

 - Windermere

10 BLACKPOOL PLEASURE BEACH

Blackpool seafront

Blackpool is the entertainment and family-fun capital of the north. Every conceivable form of holiday entertainment is on offer, from fun fairs, arcades, parks, theatres and waxworks to the famous Blackpool Tower. The Pleasure Beach is home to the tallest, fastest roller coaster in the world - the 'Big One'. Added

to all this are the miles of safe, sandy beaches and, of course, the world-famous illuminations.

 - Blackpool

11 LAUREL & HARDY MUSEUM

4c Upper Brook Street, Ulverston

Stan Laurel, the thin one of the Laurel and Hardy comedy duo, was born at Ulverston in 1890, and the town now houses a small museum to commemorate both of these popular comedy heroes. It contains a collection of personal items associated with the famous duo, and includes screenings of some of the 105 films they made.
Open daily all year, except Christmas Day.
📞 01229 582292

- Ulverston

12 DALTON LEISURE CENTRE

Chapel Street, Dalton-in-Furness

This community-run leisure facility is ideal for a family day out, specialising in children's activities. There is a large leisure pool with frog slide, saunas, squash courts, a gymnasium, children's rides and video games. There is also a pool-side café and viewing area.
Open daily, all year. 📞 01229 463125

- Dalton-in-Furness

13 LAKELAND WILDLIFE OASIS

Hale, located on the A6, 2.5 miles (4 km) south of Milnthorpe

The Lakeland Wildlife Oasis is half zoo and half museum. As well as live animals, there are imaginative hands-on audiovisual displays about the world of wildlife. Many unusual animals are also featured, such as poison-arrow frogs and flying foxes. There are walk-through enclosures to explore and picnic areas are also provided.
Open daily all year, except Christmas. 📞 015395 63027

- Arnside

Rainy days

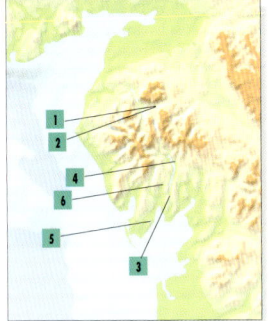

With so many of Lakeland's attractions situated out-of-doors, you might be grateful for these suggestions on indoor places to visit when it rains - which it often does in the Lake District due to the mountainous terrain. With so many interesting places to choose from, however, a rainy day need not pose a problem.

1 'CARS OF THE STARS' MOTOR MUSEUM

Standish Street, Keswick

This quirky museum started out as the personal collection of a local dentist and includes several cars used in the James Bond films, as well as James Herriot's car and Del Boy's Reliant van, from the series *Only Fools and Horses*. Other exhibits include the original Batmobile, Chitty Chitty Bang Bang and Noddy's car! Open daily, Easter-New Year. 017687 73757

- Penrith

2 CUMBERLAND PENCIL MUSEUM

Southey Works, Cording Mill Lane, Keswick

Here's somewhere unusual you might like to visit on a wet day: the Pencil Museum at Keswick. Owned by Rexel and still a fully-operational factory, the museum has various displays of machinery, past and present, used in the manufacture of pencils, with audio-visual displays to explain the manufacturing process. Graphite, used to provide the 'lead' in modern pencils, is found locally and is the reason for the factory being sited here. The first pencil was made at Keswick as long ago as the 1550s. Open daily, all year. 017687 73626

- Penrith

3 AQUARIUM OF THE LAKES

Lakeside, Newby Bridge

Embark upon a journey of discovery and meet the inhabitants of the Lakes in the 'Aquarium of the Lakes'. Take a voyage along a typical Lakeland river, following its course from mountain-top to sea. There are over 30 displays, including an underwater glass

tunnel, the largest collection of freshwater fish in Britain, otters and marine exhibits from the Irish Sea, including rays and octopuses. Open daily all year, except Christmas Day. 015395 30153

- Grange-over-Sands

4 BROCKHOLE VISITORS' CENTRE

Situated on the main A591, between Windermere and Ambleside

Brockhole is the main Visitor Centre of the Lake District National Park. Located in a beautiful and distinctive building (formerly a house) and set in delightful gardens, it is administered by the Park authorities and contains a number of imaginative displays, outlining the work of the Park and local people and the natural history of this spectacular region. Open daily, all year. 015394 46601

- Windermere

6 HILL TOP

Near Sawrey, on the B5285

The charming farmhouse at Hill Top, at Near Sawrey, was once the home of Beatrix Potter. She wrote several of her famous children's books whilst living there, the settings of which will be immediately recognisable by many of her most avid fans. The house and its surroundings are now in the care of the National Trust, who still farm the land, and also keep the house very much as it was in her day. The house now contains a wealth of Beatrix Potter memorabilia

5 CUMBRIA CRYSTAL

Lightburn Road, Ulverston

Cumbria Crystal offers something different for a rainy day, a rare opportunity to tour a specialist factory making fine lead crystal stemware and giftware. Take the factory tour and watch craftsmen using traditional methods of glass-blowing and cutting. Afterwards, you can browse in the factory shop, where a wide range of pieces are offered for sale at greatly discounted prices.
Open daily, all year. Closed Sun.
01229 584400

Some - Ulverston

to explore. Note that because of the large number of visitors, a timed entry system operates. Open on certain days, Apr Oct. 015394 36269

- Windermere

LAKESIDE RESORTS

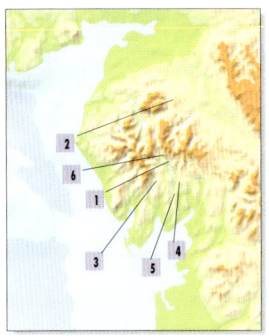

The Lakeside resorts have a special charm all of their own. Less commercial or hurried than the coastal resorts of the region, these towns make ideal bases from which to tour the Lake District, offering every convenience and comfort for the modern traveller and providing a memorable holiday experience.

1 AMBLESIDE

After Windermere town itself, Ambleside is the most popular resort in the environs of Lake Windermere. Situated at the heart of Lakeland, it is a favourite both with hardened fell walkers (who use it as a convenient base) and with day-trippers, who want to get as much as possible out of a brief trip to the Lakes. Despite the crowds of high summer, it remains a delightful little town, with several inns and restaurants and a wide variety of accommodation on offer.

P ♿ 🍴 ⛴ - Windermere

2 POOLEY BRIDGE

For many people the most beautiful of the Lakes is Ullswater, with its unspoilt shores and graceful serpentine outline. Similarly, Pooley Bridge, situated at the northern edge of this lake, is considered by some as the ultimate Lakeside resort. This delightful village of quaint streets used to be home to

a regular fish market when locals earned their living from the waters of the lake. Now they earn their living from visitors to the lake. The village is situated a little way inland, but boats tie up at a pier on the shore to take visitors on a cruise of the lake.

P ♿ 🍴 ⛴ - Penrith

3 CONISTON

The small town of Coniston lies about half a mile from the shores of Coniston Water. Now earning its living mostly from the tourist trade, it used to be a copper mining town. Several of the old mine workings can still be seen in the vicinity. Boat and ferry trips are available on the lake, while Coniston itself boasts excellent visitor facilities. Its location just away from the lake shore has preserved the unique character of the setting, whilst at the same time attending to the needs of tourists.

P ♿ 🍴 ⛴ - Ulverston

4 WINDERMERE

Windermere is the premier resort town of the Lake District, situated about mid-way along the eastern bank of the lake of the same name. For most visitors, Windermere *is* the Lake District. It is the largest of the lakes in this region and the most easily accessible, with good road and rail links. The town has grown, especially in recent years, and is the commercial centre of the Lakes, offering visitors every conceivable attraction, with water sports, lake cruises, cafés, restaurants and a myriad of hotels. Yet, despite its obvious popularity, it is still largely unspoilt and as an added bonus, offers commanding views of the mountains all around.

P WC ⚑ ♿   🚂 - Windermere

5 BOWNESS-ON-WINDERMERE

Bowness is now really a suburb of Windermere town, but it has a charm all of its own, with its quaint streets and delightful lakeside setting. Many of the waterside attractions of the lake are accessible from Bowness and a regular ferry service operates to the opposite shore. Most of the holiday trade, with its cafés, shops and attractions, is centred on Bowness rather than Windermere itself. Until 1847, Windermere was known as Birthwaite, but was renamed

after the nearby lake to give the new railway station there a more romantic-sounding name.

P WC ⚑ ♿   🚂 - Windermere

6 GRASMERE

The village of Grasmere lies at the northern edge of the small lake of the same name. It is very popular in the height of the season because of its associations with the poet William Wordsworth. He lived at two houses nearby; at Rydal Mount, where he died in 1850, and at Dove Cottage (now a museum), at the southern end of the village, where he lived from 1799 until 1808. In August each year the Grasmere Sports are held, England's equivalent to the Highland Games, when crowds flock from all over the district.

P WC ⚑ ♿   🚂 - Windermere

Days of adventure

The Lake District affords ample opportunities for those who want more from their holiday than walking or scenic tours. For them, an exciting world of adventure awaits, with a whole host of activities on offer to fire the imagination or generate adrenaline.

1 MOUNTAIN CLIMBING

While fell walking can be a lot more exciting than many realise, for the more adventurous, there is nothing quite like the exhilaration of mountain climbing, pitting one's wits and skills against the elements. Do not be misled by the apparent lack of stature of British mountains, however - there are many impressive and magnificent climbs to be had in the Lake District, comparable with anything you will find abroad. It is recommended that you never climb alone and only go with recognised groups, such as Outward Bound, Watermillock, Penrith.
☎ 0990 134227 (Outward Bound Trust). For more details about climbing, contact the British Mountaineering Council, 177-179 Burton Road, Manchester ☎ 0161 4454747.

2 WATER SPORTS

For many, the attraction of the Lakes is not just the stunning scenery, but also the opportunity to practise water sports on relatively safe waters and without the problems of tides, which are a feature of coastal resorts. Windermere, on a summer's day, can look positively Mediterranean, with all manner of sailing and motor craft bobbing up and down on the lake. The largest lakes afford the best opportunities for water sports, ranging from the genteel art of rowing to the exhilarating experience of water-skiing, powerboating or windsurfing. Several centres in the lakes offer a wide range of activities.
Try Derwentwater Marina, Portinscale ☎ 017687 72912.

3 BALLOON TRIPS

What better way to see the beauties of Lakeland than from a hot-air balloon, floating leisurely and effortlessly over this marvellous landscape. It is the only way to fully appreciate the majesty of the setting. Passengers are normally expected to help raise and lower the balloon before jumping into the basket and you never know quite where you will finish up as you follow the thermals. Flights normally take the place in the early morning and evening, when most of the crowds have gone and you have this whole incredible landscape to yourself. Several companies operate balloon flights in Lakeland, including High Adventure R.M. Travel, at Bowness-on-Windermere 📞 015394 47599.

4 PONY TREKKING

The Lake District provides some of the finest riding and pony trekking country in England. It is also amongst the wildest, so is generally

only recommended for experienced riders, especially in the more exposed and rugged high fells. To ride along a lonely mountain track can feel like stepping back into the past, when horses provided the main mode of transport.

For more details about riding in the Lakeland, contact the Cumbria Bridleways Society
📞 01966 33188.

i If you would like to try something a little more adventurous (like paragliding. off-road driving or white water rafting, for example) but have never done it before - or even if you don't know which activity you would like to try, then Acorn Activities might be for you. They offer a range of outdoor pursuits to suit people of all ages and abilities
📞 01432 830083

5 MOUNTAIN BIKING

Where else but in the Lake District are mountain bikes truly at home, on the terrain they were designed for. Some visitors will undoubtedly bring their own bikes with them, but for others who might like to try their skills at this exacting sport for the first time, there are plenty of places to hire bikes. For the energetic, there is also the 259-mile (416 km) Cumbria Cycle Way which completely encircles the county, mostly on minor roads, with some off-road sections. In the interests of conservation, however, please use designated tracks (there are plenty of them) to avoid adding to the damage already caused by thoughtless cyclists to often fragile mountain landscapes. You may also like to try the two Cycle Routes that accompany this guide.

For more information on routes available, telephone the nearest Tourist Information Centres - see page 42. The following establishments also provide cycle hire: Keswick Motor Co., Lake Road,
📞 017687 72064;
and Eden Cyclo Tours,
Unit 8, Redhills, Penrith
📞 01768 899950.

16 UNUSUAL DAYS OUT

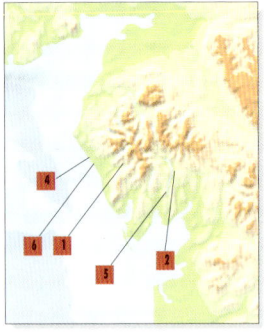

It can sometimes be difficult to find activities that appeal to the whole family when on holiday. On these occasions, doing something just a little bit different is often the solution - from a gentle Lakeland cruise to a tour round a nuclear power station, there's plenty to choose from!

1 HARDKNOTT PASS & ROMAN FORT

Hardknott Pass is one of the most spectacular roads in England, with several hairpin bends and 1:3 gradients as it climbs an incredible 1,000 ft (305 m) in a little over a mile (2 km). Surrounded by high fells, it is a wonderful setting and one recognised early on by the Romans, who built a fort there on the heights commanding the pass, remains of which can still be seen. A good way to see the pass and fort (particularly in summer when the road is busy) is to leave your car at Ravenglass and take the light railway to Eskdale, from where the fort is about a 3-mile (5 km) walk. Hardknott Castle Roman Fort (English Heritage) is freely accessible all year.

P 🚂 - Ravenglass, or Eskdale

2 LAKE CRUISES

One of the finest ways to see the Lakes and appreciate the beauty and grandeur of their setting, is to take a lake cruise. Several of the larger lakes offer a variety of cruises, from small pleasure boats to large cruisers and steamboats. The cruises can be used for sightseeing only or as ferry services, to get to other parts of the Lakes. The more adventurous may want to hire a small self-drive motor boat or a rowing boat and take themselves off on a voyage of discovery.

Open daily, all year. Windermere Lake Cruises offer a variety of alternatives.

📞 015395 31188 or 015394 43360

P 🚻 🍴 ♿ 🚂 - Windermere

3 'MOUNTAIN GOAT' MINI COACH TOURS

For days of true 'high adventure', that combine scenic beauties of the wildest parts of Lakeland, visits to top tourist attractions, walks and boat trips, with refreshments and meals included - all with the added bonus of letting someone else do

the driving - why not try a mini-bus excursion. Several companies, including Mountain Goat, operate half-day and whole-day tours, special packages and short breaks. They cater for all tastes and for people of all abilities.

📞 015394 45161

4 SELLAFIELD VISITOR CENTRE
Signposted off the A595

The Visitor Centre at Sellafield nuclear power station is one of the top tourist attractions in Cumbria. Located on the coast near Seascale, it lies just outside the Lake District National Park. It was originally set up to help the public become better informed about the nuclear industry, and has grown from there. Regular tours of the power station are held and there are many interactive displays on the modern power industry.
Open daily all year, except Christmas Day.
☎ 019467 27027

🅿 ℹ 🍴 ♿   🚆 - Sellafield

5 FELL FOOT PARK
Newby Bridge

Although a road skirts the eastern bank of Lake Windermere, there are only a few places where there is public access to the shore. One of the best of these is Fell Foot Park, an 18-acre National Trust site offering safe bathing, boat hire, family fun, tea room, shop and picnics. A regular foot-passenger ferry service operates across the

lake to Lakeside, which is also the terminus of the Haverthwaite-Lakeside restored steam railway. Why not combine a rail journey and lake cruise with your visit to Fell Foot Park. Open daily, all year.
☎ 015395 31273 🅿 ℹ 🍴 ♿
🚆 - Windermere/Grange-over-Sands

CUMBERLAND & WESTMORLAND WRESTLING

Wrestling has been a popular sport since prehistoric times. In Cumberland, a particular form of wrestling has developed in which the two opponents start the match by clasping one another over the shoulder, in a kind of bear hug, rather than standing opposite one another. The object is for each opponent to try to throw the other to the ground without releasing their grip. There are several local variations, including Westmorland wrestling. The sport is still very popular and can regularly be seen at country shows throughout Cumbria, such as at Grasmere, Ambleside and Keswick.

6 RAVENGLASS & ESKDALE RAILWAY
Ravenglass

If you fancy something just that little bit different, why not take a ride on the Ravenglass & Eskdale light railway, known affectionately as 'La'al Ratty'. Originally built to carry iron ore from the mines in Eskdale to the coastal ports, it started carrying passengers as early as 1876. In all there are seven stations along its 7 mile (11 km) length, which are used by neighbouring villages as a local transport system. Several circular walks have been devised, using the railway as a convenient link, enabling you to combine a journey with a walk into the fells, without the need to take your car. There is also a railway museum at Ravenglass and a pub, *The Ratty Arms*, serving real ale. Open daily, all year. ☎ 01229 717171

🅿 ℹ 🍴 ♿   🚆 - Ravenglass

18 HIDDEN DELIGHTS

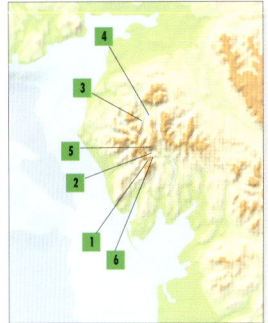

Despite its popularity as a holiday destination, the Lake District remains unspoilt and contains some of the most beautiful landscapes in England. Those in search of peace and quiet do not have to venture far from the main resorts to find it, and can take advantage of the opportunity to escape from the hustle and bustle of everyday life.

1 BLEA TARN

Blea Tarn is a delightful spot, best reached from the minor road that passes through Little Langdale Valley, taking the right fork to Side Gates. Blea Tarn lies to the left of the road and to reach it you must park at a car park on the opposite side of the road and take the footpath. It is a lovely spot for a picnic, overlooked by fells all around, with tree plantations and a beautiful display of rhododendrons at the shore.

🅿 ♿ - Little Langdale 🚌 - Windermere

2 RIVER BRATHAY & ELTERWATER

From Skelwith Bridge, the River Brathay can be followed, first at high level and then along the bank itself to Elterwater, a small and attractive lake in the shadow of the Langdale Pikes. The path continues

northwestwards to Elterwater village, this time following the Great Langdale Beck.

🅿 ♿ 🍴 - Elterwater and Skelwith Bridge 🚌 - Windermere

3 CAT BELLS

The charmingly named Cat Bells, along the western shores of Derwentwater, is a great favourite with those who want to experience the achievement of fell-walking in a gentler way. Cat Bells, although of modest height, looks grand and commanding, with fine views of Derwentwater and the surrounding fells. Easily reached from Littletown or Hawes End (where there is a car park) it is a delightful walk.

🅿 ♿ 🚌 - Penrith

4 ASHNESS BRIDGE

Ashness Bridge, with the distant view of the Skiddaw range of hills beyond, is one of the most celebrated views of Lakeland and graces many calendars and chocolate box tops. The scene is perfection itself, with all the component parts lined up obligingly for the camera, but, surprisingly,

the scene is seldom actually visited. Most people pass over the bridge and admire the view, perhaps pausing for a quick photo. However, there is parking nearby and National Trust land overlooking Derwentwater that is well worth exploring on foot.

P 🚂 - Penrith

5 SKELWITH FORCE

Most visitors to Great Langdale head straight for the valley itself after leaving Ambleside, perhaps pausing at the little village of Skelwith Bridge, with its visitor facilities. But nearby, and often overlooked by those with busy itineraries, is Skelwith Force, another majestic waterfall. Just beyond the village there is parking and access to the River Brathay. The waterfall is reached by crossing an abandoned mill race.

P 🚻 ♿ 🍴 - at Skelwith Bridge
🚂 - Windermere

APPLEBY HORSE FAIR

The Appleby Horse Fair is the largest, and most riotous, fair of its kind in Britain, where horse dealers traditionally meet to buy and sell horses. It is not a fair in the modern sense of the word, but more an annual gathering, particularly of gypsies and travellers, who meet just outside the town on Fair (or Gallows) Hill. Festivities are held over a week in early June, with buyers and sellers putting the horses through their paces. Although the fairs are more restrained than they once were, it can be mayhem, so be warned; exciting it may be, but it's not for the faint-hearted!

6 LITTLE LANGDALE

Although Little Langdale lacks the scenic delights of its grander, and more popular near-neighbour, Great Langdale, the valley of Little Langdale has much more charm. It is certainly quieter and more peaceful. There are numerous disused quarries hereabouts and not to be missed is Slater's Bridge, built by, and for the use of, the quarrymen. It is reckoned to be one of the prettiest bridges in Lakeland. The side valley of Greenburn is also a must to explore.

P 🚻 🍴 - at Little Langdale ♿   🚂 - Windermere

Hidden Delights

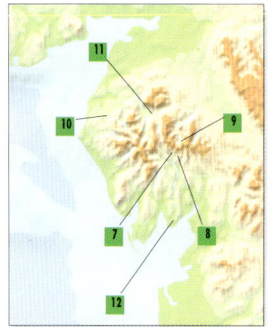

7 HIGH SWEDEN BRIDGE

One of the delights of Lakeland often missed by ramblers determined to walk the famous Fairfield Horseshoe ridge walk, is the curiously named High Sweden Bridge. The bridge crosses Scandale Beck, a fast-flowing mountain stream that tumbles over rocks and through deep ravines in the beautiful Rydal Valley. It is a classic pack-horse bridge of ancient construction and timeless in its appeal. To reach it, park in Ambleside and walk up the steep Kirkstone Road. A signed lane, that soon becomes little more than a stoney track, leads off to the left.

`P WC t - in Ambleside`   `- Windermere`

CUMBERLAND SAUSAGES

There are several local recipes that are a speciality of the region, such as Cumberland sausages, still made locally by butchers in the time-honoured way. They are much larger and more savoury than usual sausages, so why not treat yourself to a full English breakfast with Cumberland sausages while you are here!

8 STOCK GHYLL FORCE

Along a small side road leading out of Ambleside, behind the Salutation Hotel, can be found, after a very short distance, one of the most impressive waterfalls in Lakeland, Stock Ghyll Force. Surrounded by trees, the Stock Ghyll Stream tumbles down over boulders in two impressive cascades, falling a total of

60 ft (19 m) into a rocky hollow. In peak season it can be busy, but it is a magnificent sight and should be savoured at leisure. Try and visit out of season if you can.

`P WC t - in Ambleside`

`- Windermere`

9 KIRKSTONE PASS

The Kirkstone Pass is one of the wilder, more desolate aspects of Lakeland. The scenery all around is impressive, but very remote. The A592 makes its way directly northwards from Windermere. A minor road from Ambleside, known as 'The Struggle', meets the main road at the Kirkstone Pass Inn, where there is also a lookout point. The pass takes its name from a huge boulder, known as the Kirk Stone, one of many that have tumbled down the hillsides, and is now a familiar landmark. From the inn and lookout point, several footpaths take the more adventurous into this wild landscape.

`P WC t & - at the inn and lookout`

`- Windermere`

10 LOWESWATER

Loweswater is one of the smaller lakes, located just inside the National Park boundary (in the northwest corner) far away from the main tourist regions and often overlooked. It is owned by the National Trust and surrounded by beautiful fells. Because of its location it is also one of the least spoilt of the lakes, with no evidence

of commercial exploitation whatsoever. Once, all the lakes must have looked like this.

P WC & ¶◎¶ - at nearby hotel

🚂 - Workington

11 VALE OF ST. JOHN

Just to the north of Thirlmere, where the A591 goes on to Keswick, a minor road (the B5322) forks right at Legburthwaite and heads into the tranquil Vale of St. John. After the hustle and bustle of the main road, all is suddenly peace and quiet, with glorious views. The first few miles are dominated by towering crags that rise up on both sides of the valley. St. John's Beck roughly parallels the road, and about halfway along the valley to the left is a side road which leads to the lovely church of St. John, a beautiful and tranquil spot.

P & 🚂 - Penrith

KENDAL MINT CAKE

Another firm favourite, especially with visitors, is Kendal Mint Cake. It is a hard, mint-flavoured sugar slab, still made to a local recipe and available throughout the Lake District - although people from Kendal will tell you that theirs is by far the best! It is much-loved by walkers because of its high sugar content, which gives them extra energy when walking the fells.

12 CARTMEL

The delightful village of Cartmel nestles in a shallow valley, by Lakeland standards, dominated by Cartmel Priory. It was founded in 1188 by William Marshall. In addition to endowing it with lands, Marshall also decreed that the Priory should provide a priest for the people of Cartmel village, an act which saved the buildings from being destroyed at the Dissolution. Situated south of the main tourist areas surrounding the Lakes, Cartmel is something of a gem.

P WC ¶◎¶ & 🚂 - Cark

Literary Landscapes

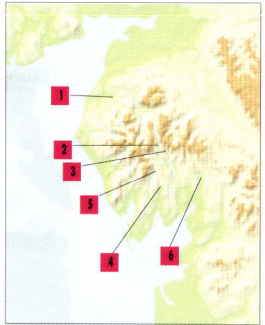

Probably no other region in Britain has inspired as many writers as the Lake District. It is a landscape that haunts the imagination and appeases the senses like no other. No wonder, then, that some of our greatest poets, novelists and essayists have been drawn to its beguiling beauty over the centuries. Follow us now in the footsteps of some of our greatest writers.

'I Wandered Lonely As A Cloud'

William Wordsworth (1770-1850) has become famous as one of our best-loved Romantic poets. Many of the beautiful lines he composed were inspired by the Lakeland scenery. Wordsworth is usually cited as the central figure in the company of artists and poets who frequently visited his home. Recent research would suggest, however, that his sister Dorothy, not only inspired and encouraged him, but may even have penned some of the lines attributed to him herself. The Wordsworths were often in the company of fellow poet Samuel Taylor Coleridge, who lived nearby at Greta Hall, Keswick.

1 COCKERMOUTH
William Wordsworth's birthplace

Unlike several other Lakeland writers who were 'off-comers', or outsiders, who adopted the area as their home, Wordsworth was born here, at Cockermouth. His birthplace (Wordsworth House, National Trust) can still be seen in the Main Street, a small and friendly house still furnished in the style of the period.
Open Mon.-Fri, Apr.-Oct. ☎ 01900 824805

🅿 WC 🚂 - Penrith

2 GRASMERE
Dove Cottage

This is the house most associated with Wordsworth and is also considered by many to be the most attractive. Dove Cottage was Wordsworth's home from 1799-1808. The house is run by the Wordsworth Trust as a museum and contains many unique items associated with the great poet, including many books, paintings and manuscripts. The delightful gardens are also open. The house dates from the 1600s and was originally a public house.
Open daily all year, except 24-26 Dec. and 11 Jan.-7 Feb. ☎ 015394 35544

🅿 WC 🍴 ♿ 🚂 - Windermere

3 AMBLESIDE
Rydal Mount

Following a brief spell at Grasmere Rectory, Wordsworth came to Rydal Mount in 1813 and made it his family home. It incorporates a 16th-century farmer's cottage at its core, with many additions, and has been carefully preserved by its present owners (descendants of the poet) to reflect how it would have looked when Wordsworth was in residence. Appointed Poet Laureate in 1843, Wordsworth died at Rydal Mount in 1850.
Open daily all year, except Tues. between Nov. & Feb.
☎ 015394 33002

🅿 WC 🚂 - Windermere

4 BEATRIX POTTER
Hill Top, Near Sawrey

For many, the name most associated with the Lake District is Beatrix Potter, the perennially popular writer of children's books and creator of Peter Rabbit, Mrs. Tiggywinkle and a host of other favourite characters. An 'off-comer' (outsider), she was born in London in 1866 and first visited the Lakes on a family holiday in 1882, returning year after year. Eventually, she moved to the Lakes, after commuting for several years. Her home, Hill Top, is now a museum and is one of the most visited attractions in Lakeland (a timed entry system operates). Having tried unsuccessfully to get her children's stories published, Beatrix Potter published 'The Tale of Peter Rabbit and Mr. McGregor's Garden' herself, in 1901; the rest, as they say, is history. The author used much of the money from the sale of her books to purchase land in the Lake District (over 4,000 acres), which she bequeathed to the National Trust when she died in 1943. House open Sat. - Wed., Gardens open daily, Apr.- Oct. 015394 36269 - Windermere

5 JOHN RUSKIN
Brantwood, Coniston

Brantwood is one of the most beautifully sited houses in the Lake District, with magnificent views over Coniston Water. The rambling, white-painted house was the home of John Ruskin from 1872 until his death in 1900. Ruskin was one of the foremost 'thinkers' of his time and the house is filled with his drawings, watercolours, books, furniture and personal items. There are numerous literary and artistic works associated with Ruskin on display throughout the house, demonstrations and a video programme. Open daily, Mar.-Nov.; Wed.-Sun. during winter months. 015394 41396 - Windermere

6 WAINWRIGHT
Kendal

A more recent but no less celebrated writer associated with the Lake District is Alfred Wainwright. Born in Blackburn in 1907, Wainwright, as he liked to be known, or simply A.W., moved to Kendal in 1941, becoming Borough Treasurer in 1948. Between 1952-65 he compiled seven guidebooks to the Lakeland fells, the first four of which he published himself. Everything was hand-drawn and hand-written, and the books quickly became classics, avidly sought after and read by all lovers of Lakeland. During his retirement he wrote over 40 more guide books and took part in several B.B.C. documentaries based on his walks. His inimitable, pithy, yet humorous books are unique and are far and away the most successful ever written on Lakeland. He died in 1991.

HERITAGE OF THE LAKE DISTRICT

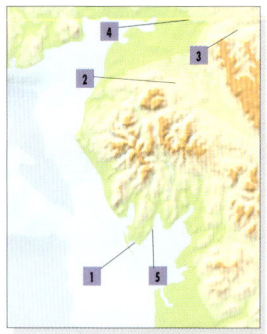

The Lake District is rich in history and architectural heritage. There are numerous castles and other fortifications dotted about the landscape, because this region has always been in dispute in the border warfare between England and Scotland. There are few great houses in this remote corner of the country, but there are considerable monastic remains.

1 FURNESS ABBEY
Signposted from the centre of Barrow-in-Furness

Furness Abbey, near Barrow-in-Furness, is one of the most substantial monastic remains in northern England. First built in 1147 by Cistercian monks, the abbey grew to become one of the richest in the north, with several large land-holdings in the Cumbrian fells. The monks controlled a number of farms, set up trade routes with Ireland and reclaimed large areas of marshland from the sea. The abbey was deserted following the Dissolution in 1542. Open daily all year, except 25-26 Dec. and 1st Jan. 01229 823420

P - Barrow-in-Furness

The more adventurous may wish to walk the 33-mile (53 km) Cistercian Way, using public roads and footpaths linking several monastic sites in the little-known area along the northern shores of Morecambe Bay.

2 HUTTON-IN-THE-FOREST
Penrith, 3 miles (5 km) west from exit 41 of M6, on the B5305

This beautiful historic house on the northeastern edge of the Lake District is surrounded by the medieval forest of Inglewood. It has been the home of the Inglewood family since 1605. Hutton-in-the-Forest was originally a humble Pele tower, built in the 14th century as a refuge against Scottish raids. Succeeding generations have added to and improved the range of buildings ever since. There are good collections of furniture and fine arts from all periods. The house sits in magnificent grounds, with a 1730s walled garden, large herbaceous collection, topiary and a woodland walk. House open daily, Easter and May-Sept. Gardens open all year.

017684 84449   - Penrith

3 HADRIAN'S WALL

The western terminus of Hadrian's Wall was at Solway Firth, over 73 miles (117 km) from Wallsend, in Northumberland, on the east coast. The entire length of the wall has now been declared a World Heritage Site by UNESCO and considerable stretches of the wall survive, measuring as high as 10 ft (3 m) in places. The associated earthwork defences also survive and each year more and more of the wall is uncovered and preserved by archaeologists. The wall crosses some of the wildest and most dramatic scenery in northern England. Built by the Romans from about AD 121, under Emperor Hadrian, the wall was intended to mark the northernmost limits of their Empire and protect England from Scottish raids. Several forts were built at intervals along the length of the wall, many of which still survive. Substantial Roman remains can be seen at Banks and Birdoswald, an ideal base from which to explore the wall.

P WC ¶ & 🚌 - Brampton

4 CARLISLE CASTLE

Castle Way

From Roman times until the 17th century, Carlisle has always been a strategic border town in the disputes between England and Scotland. The Romans fortified the town with a strong wall, replaced by the Normans 1,000 years later, who also added a castle. The mighty, well-preserved structure you see today dates mostly from the reign of Henry I (mid-12th century). The castle was used as a prison for Mary, Queen of Scots in 1568 and was attacked by Bonnie Prince Charlie in 1745. The impressive Border Regiment Museum is housed in Queen Mary's Tower. Open daily all year, closed 24-25 Dec. and 1st Jan.
☎ 01228 591880

P WC ¶ & 🚌 - Carlisle

5 GLEASTON WATER MILL

Ulverston - signposted from the A5087

An unusual day out at an authentic and atmospheric 18th-century water mill. Gleaston Water Mill dates from 1774, although it stands on the site of a much older Mill, and has been restored to full working order. The impressive water wheel is 18 ft (5.5 m) in diameter and is still used to grind corn. There are fascinating displays and tours of the mill and a shop selling products from the mill and gifts. Outside, there are farm animals, including highland cattle, pigs and several rare breeds.
Open daily all year, except Mon (and Tues in winter.) ☎ 01229 869244

P WC ¶ & 🚌 - Barrow-in-Furness

DRYSTONE WALLS

One of the features of Lakeland, as with other mountainous, moorland and high regions of the country, is the drystone walls. The walls are built from the scattered rocks and scree that lie all over the landscape here and are freely available. Different areas adopt regional variations, but basically the methods of construction are the same. They are amongst the most typical man-made landscape features of Lakeland and are more commonly used than hedges as stock barriers between fields. Typically, a drystone wall is constructed by building two outer walls of large stones, tapering inwards, with an infill of smaller stones, held together without the use of mortar.

HERITAGE OF THE LAKE DISTRICT

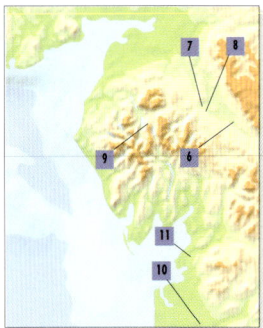

6 APPLEBY CASTLE *Boroughgate, Appleby*

Situated at the eastern edge of the Lake District, and deep in the heart of the Eden Valley, stands Appleby Castle. First built in Norman times, this beautiful fortress stands guard over the old Westmorland town of Appleby. In the 17th century, it was converted into a stately home by the Clifford family and the castle still retains many fine paintings and pieces of furniture from that period. Outside, in the 27 acres of surrounding parkland, can be seen birds, rare farm animals, falconry displays, medieval re-enactments and special events throughout the season. Open daily, Easter-end of Oct. 017683 51402

P WC & ¶ 🚌 - Appleby

7 BROUGHAM HALL
Off the B6262, Penrith

The history of the site occupied by Brougham Hall goes back to Bronze Age times. The hall is essentially a fortified manor house, dating from about 1480 (containing at its core an earlier Pele tower), with later additions. It was once owned by Lord Chancellor Brougham, who, in 1832, introduced the Parliamentary Reform Bill. Brougham

8 BROUGHAM CASTLE

1.5 miles (2 km) south of Penrith

Brougham Castle, near Penrith, is similar in appearance, and has a remarkably similar history to nearby Brough Castle. The Romans also built a fort here, known as Brocarium, though in this case the Normans chose to build their castle adjacent to the fort rather than within it, as at Brough. Lady Anne Clifford carried out an elaborate restoration programme at the castle in the 17th century. She died there in 1676, aged nearly 90. The castle afterwards fell into disrepair, though much still remains to be seen today. Open daily, Apr.-Oct. 01768 862488

P WC & 🚌 - Penrith

Hall is the largest country house project in the U.K. Admission is free, although voluntary donations are requested. Open daily all year, except Christmas Day. 01768 868184

P WC & ¶ 🚌 - Penrith

9 CASTLERIGG STONE CIRCLE

2 miles (3 km) east of Keswick

Although there are considerable Roman remains in the region north of the Lake District, the area has been settled for far longer. There are a number of prehistoric sites to be seen, including Castlerigg Stone Circle, a few miles east of Keswick. The stones were erected about

2,000 BC and are of unknown purpose, though the circle was probably used for religious ceremonies. Easily accessible from Keswick, few ancient monuments can be so dramatically sited, surrounded as it is by high mountains. Cared for by English Heritage, the Circle may be freely visited at any time.

P WC ❙❙ ♿ in Keswick 🚂 - Penrith

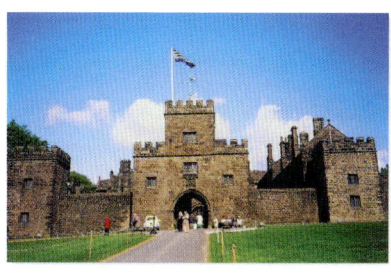

10 HOGHTON TOWER

On the A675, 6 miles (10 km) east of Preston

Some miles south of the Lake District is Hoghton Tower, one of the most dramatic looking houses in the north of England. The ancestral home of the Hoghton family since Norman times, it began as a hilltop fortified manor house. The present house, the third to occupy the site, was built between 1560-5. The magnificent Banqueting Hall is where Shakespeare is believed to have started his working life and was also the supposed setting in which James I dubbed the loin of beef at table 'Sir Loin', in 1617. Open July-Sept, Mon.-Thur., plus Sun. and Bank Holidays. 📞 01254 852986

P WC ❙❙ 🚂 - Preston

11 LANCASTER CASTLE

Castle Hill

Lancaster Castle, just east of Morecambe Bay and to the south of Lakeland, is one of the most important and complete castles in the north-west of England. It is also unique in that it is still used for its original purpose: much of the castle is still both a court of law and a prison. When the prison closes at the Millennium, more of these extensive and fascinating buildings will be opened to the public. Already on view are the magnificent Shire Hall, the Crown Court and Grand Jury Room and the dungeons. The castle, which was first built in 1093, stands on the site of a Roman fort. Open daily, Mar.-Dec.

📞 01524 64998 P WC ❙❙ ♿ in Lancaster town 🚂 - Lancaster

BEAUTIFUL GARDENS

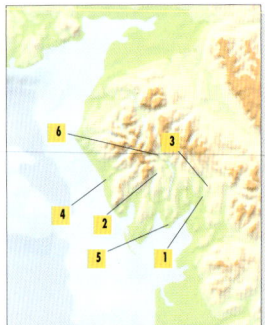

It is difficult to imagine how nature could be improved upon in the Lake District, but the area plays host to a stunning array of truly beautiful gardens to augment the hand of nature. Using the wild and rugged fells as a backdrop, the more formal plantings of the gardens here are an attraction of Lakeland well worth seeing.

1 LEVENS HALL & GARDENS
Kendal

Levens Hall is a magnificent Elizabethan mansion built around a 13th-century Pele tower and surrounded by lovely gardens. The house is open to visitors and contains fine collections of Jacobean furniture, paintings and the earliest English patchwork, dating from about 1708. The award-winning gardens are stunning in all seasons and contain a topiary garden of world-renown. They were first laid out in 1694 and have been lovingly extended ever since. The house and gardens, which are just five minutes from junction 36 on the M6, are reputedly haunted by several ghosts. Open daily, Apr.-Oct. 015395 60321

- Oxenholme

2 BRANTWOOD
Off the B5285 at Coniston

Brantwood has over 30 acres of magnificent gardens, contained within an overall area of 250 acres of woodland, meadows and moorland. The gardens were originally laid out by John Ruskin and are currently being restored to his designs, including the famous Harbour Walk and Professor's Garden, where Ruskin experimented with native plants. There are several different gardens to see and also a nature trail. A conservationist well ahead of his time, Ruskin foretold of the 'greenhouse effects' on the environment, over 100 years ago. Open all year, 15 Mar.-15 Nov. daily; Winter opening, Wed.-Sun. only. 015394 41396

- Windermere

3 SIZERGH CASTLE & GARDENS
Near Kendal

Sizergh, now owned by the National Trust, is famous for its fine furnishings and beautiful gardens, including an extensive rock garden and many fine trees, with views over the surrounding countryside. It has been the family home of the Strickland family since 1239.

Open most afternoons, Apr.-Oct. 015395 60070

- Kendal

4 MUNCASTER CASTLE, GARDENS & OWL CENTRE

Ravenglass

Situated in 77 acres of fine woodland and rhododendron gardens, the 14th-century castle at Muncaster commands stunning views over the western Lakeland fells. The gardens were first laid out in the 1780s and the first rhododendrons planted in 1840. A special feature of the gardens is the World Owl Trust, which cares for over 40 different species of owl.

During the season, a conservation talk and bird display is given each day, weather permitting. Castle open Mar.-Nov., Sun.-Fri. Gardens and Owl Centre open daily, all year. ☎ 01229 717614

P WC ♿ 🍴 🚂 - Ravenglass

5 HOLKER HALL & GARDENS

Cark-in-Cartmel, Grange-over-Sands

Holker Hall, near Cartmel, is unusual among stately homes today in that visitors are free to wander around the rooms at leisure, without the usual ropes and barriers, which makes it feel much more of a home instead of a museum. The house is surrounded by over 25 acres of magnificent grounds, with formal gardens, beautiful herbaceous collections and woodland walks. The hall and gardens also play host to the Lakeland Motor Museum (see page 8), so there should be something for all the family here.
Open daily, Apr.-Oct. ☎ 015395 58328

P WC ♿ 🍴 🚂 - Cark

6 RYDAL MOUNT

Grasmere Road, 1.5 miles (2 km) from Ambleside

The gardens at Wordsworth's last home, Rydal Mount, are designed on a human scale rather than the grandiose schemes often seen at larger stately homes. Wordsworth was himself a keen landscape gardener and his sister, Dorothy, loved to tend the gardens. The garden seen today is very much as they left it. Contained within its four acres are terraces, rockeries, many rare shrubs and, of course, a carpet of daffodils and bluebells in Spring.
Open daily all year, except Tues., between Nov. & Feb.
☎ 015394 33002

P WC 🚂 - Windermere

Museums & Galleries

The Lake District is well-served with museums, from traditional local-interest museums to modern state-of-the-art displays. Many now offer audio and visual displays with hands-on facilities and computer programs, which really bring the subjects to life, making them ideal places to visit with children on rainy days, or to escape the crowds of the main resorts.

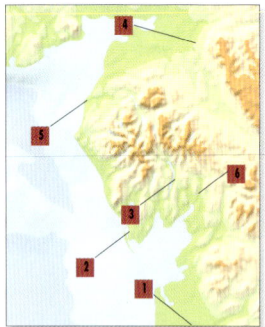

1 HARRIS MUSEUM & ART GALLERY

Market Square, Preston

This museum and art gallery is housed in a magnificent building, built in 1893 in neo-classical style. Entrance is free and special events are housed on a regular basis throughout the year. There are important collections of decorative art and of special note is the Egyptian Balcony, containing atmospheric views of Egyptian scenes painted in the early 1900s. Open Mon.-Sat., all year.

📞 01772 257112   P ♿ 🚌 - Preston

2 DOCK MUSEUM

North Road, Barrow-in-Furness

Opened only in 1994, the Dock Museum is a spectacular modern museum built over a Victorian graving dock. The displays trace the development of Barrow from a tiny 19th-century hamlet to the biggest iron and steel centre in the world and a major ship-building town. Facilities include a

3 STEAMBOAT MUSEUM

Rayrigg Road, Bowness-on-Windermere

This museum of Lake-craft was opened in 1977 by H.R.H. the Prince of Wales. Originally the private collection of George Pattinson, included amongst the exhibits are 'Dolly', the oldest mechanically-powered boat in the world still in full-working order, and the original steam-yacht used in the film 'Swallows & Amazons'. Located right on the lake shore, the museum is dedicated to preserve, restore and interpret Windermere's nautical heritage. Open daily, Mar.-Oct. 📞 015394 45565

landscaped site with adventure playground. Open all year, Wed.-Sun.
📞 01229 894444

P ♿ 🍴 🚌 - Barrow-in-Furness

P ♿ 🍴 🚌 - Windermere

4 TULLIE HOUSE MUSEUM & ART GALLERY

Castle Street, Carlisle

Tullie House is an award-winning museum and art gallery that has recently undergone a £5.5 million refurbishment programme. There are many interactive and hands-on displays. The museum tells the often turbulent story of Carlisle's history. Experience a day in the Cumbrian countryside, stroll down a Roman street, walk along Hadrian's Wall or experience the fear of the Border

5 SENHOUSE ROMAN MUSEUM

The Battery, Maryport

The Senhouse Roman Museum is housed in a former Naval Reserve Battery. Built in 1885, it is the only surviving building of its type in the country. The collection is the oldest in Britain and was begun in 1570 by John Senhouse, of Netherhall. It contains many sculptures and artefacts from the Roman period, many discovered in the nearby fort at Maryport (Alavna).
Open daily, all year. 01900 816168

P ♿ - Maryport

Reivers, marauding family gangs whose feuding terrorised the neighbourhood. Open daily, all year.
01228 534781

P ♿ ⛟ - Carlisle Citadel

6 KENDAL MUSEUMS

Kendal, situated in the southeast corner of Lakeland, boasts several excellent museums. The Kendal Museum, in Station Road, is perhaps the Lake District's best-kept secret, with displays on geology, natural history and archaeology, and several exhibits specially for children. Open daily, Mon.-Sat., all year. 01539 721374

P ♿

The Museum of Lakeland Life & Industry and Abbot Hall Art Gallery are both housed in Abbot Hall, in Highgate. The museum looks at 300 years of local history, concentrating especially on daily life for Cumbrians in the past. The art gallery is highly acclaimed for its changing displays and collection of British paintings. Both are situated in parkland on the banks of the River Kent, where you can walk or picnic. Open daily, Feb.-Dec.
01539 722464

P ♿ ⛟ - Oxenholme, Kendal

SCENIC SPLENDOURS

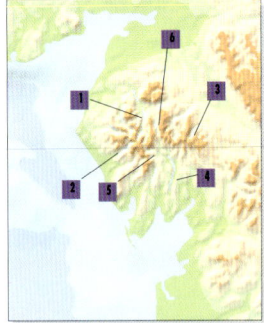

The rugged beauty of the Lake District has been attracting visitors for the last 200 years. Before that, such wild areas were considered too remote and desolate to be attractive and were termed 'wastelands'. For those wanting to stray off the beaten track and experience the true essence of Lakeland, the rewards are plentiful, and the scenery stunning.

1 DERWENTWATER & SKIDDAW

Skiddaw is reckoned by geologists to be the oldest mountain in Lakeland, formed long before volcanic activity in primeval times even began to form the other peaks. It is also the fourth highest peak - not that height has anything to do with an appreciation of beauty, as all true lovers of beautiful landscapes can testify. It is all too easy to get hung-up on numbers when dealing with mountains. Rarely can the real giants of the world be observed in their entirety anyway, so it is usually impossible to gauge the overall height. What the Lakeland mountains lack in height, they more than compensate for in scale, majesty and in grandeur. Derwentwater is one of the most attractive of the lakes, dotted with tree-clad islands and surrounded by high peaks. John Ruskin once said that the view of the lake from the Friar's Crag Viewpoint is one of the best in Europe.

P WC ⚲ & 🚆 - Penrith

2 WAST WATER

This is a place to savour and take in the views at leisure. Wastwater, at just 3 miles (5 km) long, is one of the smallest lakes, but it is also the deepest, at some 250 ft (76 m). Approached from the west, along a narrow road that hugs the lakeside, the view along the beautiful Wasdale valley is stunning. The lake is reminiscent of the Scottish Highlands and is overlooked by the tallest mountains in England, including Scafell Pike at 3,205 ft (977 m) and Great Gable.

P WC ⚲ & - Wasdale Head Hotel
🚆 - Drigg

3 ULLSWATER

Ullswater is the second largest lake in Lakeland, at 7.5 miles (12 km), and also one of the loveliest, by virtue of its graceful, serpentine curves. Daffodils growing in woodland on the shores of the lake are said to have inspired Wordsworth's classic poem of the same name. Ullswater is much less commercialised than Windermere, to which it is linked by the awe-

inspiring Kirkstone Pass, and can best be appreciated from a leisurely cruise along its waters.

P WC ⚲ & 🚆 - Windermere

4 WINDERMERE

The largest and most popular of the Lakes, Windermere is still stunningly beautiful with, at its northern end, one of the classic Lakeland views of the Langdale Pikes. Windermere sums up everyone's idea of the Lake District and, despite the crowds in high season, never fails to impress or live up to its reputation. There are some wonderful views to be had here and a trip down the length of this

magnificent lake to Lakeside is an unforgettable experience. With good road and rail links, Windermere is also the most accessible of the Lakes.

P WC ⦿ ♿   🚂 - Windermere

5 LANGDALE PIKES

There are few sights in Lakeland to compare with the Langdale Pikes. They are amongst the most imposing of the Lakeland peaks when seen distantly from Windermere, but even more so when seen closer at hand from the valley of Great Langdale. By no means the tallest, rising sheer as they do from the valley floor, they have an alpine grandeur that never fails to impress, particularly when the craggy peaks carry a mantle of snow. There are five peaks in the range, which can all be visited in a single walk, using the convenient car park at Great Langdale as a base.

P WC ⦿   🚂 - Windermere

6 THIRLMERE & HELVELLYN

The lake at Thirlmere is completely circumnavigated by roads, with a main road to the east and a minor road to the west. The lake was originally much smaller, but it was dammed at its northern end in 1879 and flooded to form a reservoir for Manchester, the first in Lakeland. Wythburn and Armboth villages, along with several farms close to the original shoreline, now lie completely submerged in the lake's depths. Overlooking the lake is Helvellyn, the third tallest peak in Lakeland at 3,116 ft (950 m) and one of the most popular fells with visitors. One of the most thrilling aspects of climbing Helvellyn is Striding Edge, an exhilarating walk along a narrow ridge, but beware of the precipitous falls to either side.

P WC ⦿   🚂 - Penrith

ABOUT TOWN

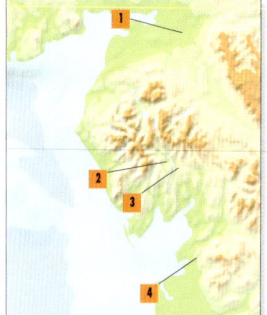

The northwest corner of England boasts several impressive towns with a range of first-class shopping and leisure facilities. There are towns of all shapes and sizes, from Lancaster, once considered part of the Lake District, and the border city of Carlisle, to the smaller, tourist-oriented towns of the Lakes, such as Windermere and Hawkshead.

1 CARLISLE

No visit to the Lake District would be complete without a trip to the ancient border-town of Carlisle, now an impressive and vibrant city with excellent facilities and shopping. It lies just north of the National Park and the main tourist areas and is perhaps all the better for that, escaping the worst of the crowds. The city is dominated by the twin symbols of medieval power, the castle (see page 25) and the cathedral, both in excellent condition. The town has often been the subject of border disputes between the English and Scots, changing hands on numerous occasions, the last time in 1745. The cathedral, originally founded in 1122, is one of the smaller English cathedrals, but a fascinating place to explore, as is the town itself, which many consider to be something of a gem in this often forgotten corner of the country.

P 🅆 🍴 ♿ 🚂 - Carlisle

2 HAWKSHEAD

Considered by some to be no more than a large village, Hawkshead has grown considerably in recent years, largely as a result of the tourist industry, and should really be considered a small town. It is included here because it provides a contrast to the larger conurbations mentioned on these pages. Despite the large influx of visitors in the summer months, Hawkshead is well worth visiting, especially as there is a large car park on the outskirts that has resulted in many of the streets becoming traffic-free. Discovering the town on foot is the only way to see this delightful place. William Wordsworth was a pupil at the grammar school between 1779-87 and the town is still very much as he would have known it. In the Middle Ages, Hawkshead was an important market town and it still retains a wealth of architectural gems. The town is a maze of narrow streets and alleyways, packed full of interesting little corners, containing gift shops, restaurants and pubs.

P 🅆 🍴 ♿ 🚂 - Windermere

3 WINDERMERE

The town of Windermere was formerly known as Birthwaite until the coming of the railway in 1847, when it was re-named in honour of the nearby lake to give the railway terminus a more romantic-sounding name. Windermere has rapidly expanded, with the advent of the tourist industry, so that it has practically joined forces with the neighbouring town of Bowness. Although Windermere is the most visited town in Lakeland, it has somehow managed to retain much of its charm and character, preserving many buildings of architectural merit and several quiet corners. The town offers everything a visitor could want, from gift shops, cafés and bars to fine restaurants, hotels and sports facilities. It owes its popularity to being the furthermost point that the railway reached within Lakeland. It is still a beautiful town and is best visited out of season to fully appreciate its charms.

P WC ⚫ ♿ 🚂 - Windermere

4 LANCASTER

Before the 1974 boundary changes, much of what is now Lakeland was part of north Lancashire. As a county town, Lancaster once featured more prominently in the affairs of Lakeland than it does now. Located just to the southeast of Morecambe Bay, this relatively small town is well worth the short excursion from the main Lakeland attractions and will amply reward your efforts. The town is dominated, as it always has been, by its castle (see page 27). There are many fine Georgian houses and a tree-lined quay, reminders of the days when Lancaster was once an important port, bigger even than Liverpool and Manchester. However, its position was not ideal and it has since declined in importance compared to its larger neighbours. The town takes its name from the Roman fort that once stood on the banks of the River Lune here: Lunecastrum.

P WC ⚫ ♿ 🚂 - Lancaster

DIARY OF EVENTS

On these two pages are listed various events and festivals that are held on a regular basis in the Lake District throughout the year. They are listed by month and contain brief details of the events. Although most are held annually, the exact dates vary from year to year so as to fall on convenient weekends or public holidays. You are advised to contact the nearest Tourist Information Centre (addresses and telephone numbers are listed on page 42 of this guide) for further information regarding dates, times and prices of admission to avoid possible disappointment, or for details of any one-off events.

APRIL

LANCASTER MARITIME FESTIVAL
Lancaster Maritime Museum, Custom House, St. George's Quay, Lancaster. *Annual event celebrating Lancaster's 'Golden Age' as an important port. Various events spread over four days.*
📞 01524 64637

VALE-OF-LUNE POINT-TO-POINT
Low Hall, Whittington, Lancashire. *Horse races, over jumps. Hounds and huntsmen.*
📞 015242 21175

MAY

BARBON HILL CLIMB
Barbon Manor, Nr. Kirkby Lonsdale. *Hill climb championship, featuring racing and sports cars against the clock.*
📞 Tourist Information Centre 015242 71437

MODEL BOAT RALLY
Windermere Steamboat Museum, Rayrigg Road, Windermere. *Model boats in action, with full-sized steamboats.*
📞 015394 45565

CONISTON WATER FESTIVAL
In and around Coniston. *Ten-day event highlighting all waterborne and shore-based activities around the lake, such as sailing, fishing, country dancing, and football.*
📞 015394 41707

JUNE

BROUGH, CUMBRIA HOUND AND TERRIER SHOW
Castle Guard, Brough. *Country dog show, also features shepherds' crooks and walking sticks.*
📞 017683 51921

WARCOP RUSH-BEARING
Warcop village. *Ancient ceremony, featuring procession through village.*
📞 017683 41249

JULY

AMBLESIDE RUSH-BEARING. *Traditional rush-bearing ceremony and procession starting from the church and moving through the town.*
📞 015394 33205

CLEATOR MOOR SPORTS
Wath Brow Sports Field, Cleator. *Sports events including athletics, cycling, and Cumberland wrestling.*
📞 01946 811656

CUMBRIA STEAM GATHERING
Cark Airfield, Flookburgh, Grange-over-Sands. *Premier steam-engine rally of the north of England, also includes stalls, fairground, circus, brass bands, etc.*
📞 015242 71584

BARBON SPRINT HILL CLIMB
Barbon Manor, Nr. Kirkby Lonsdale. *Hill climb, featuring racing and vintage motorcycles.*
📞 01539 727828

AUGUST
AMBLESIDE SPORTS
Rydal Park, Ambleside. *One of the premier traditional sports festivals of Lakeland, featuring Cumberland and Westmorland wrestling, hound trials and various field events.*
📞 015394 45531

BRITISH CLASSIC MOTORBOAT RALLY
Windermere Steamboat Museum, Rayrigg Road, Windermere. *Classic boat rally; largest gathering of traditional, motor and speedboats in the country.*
📞 015394 45565

GRASMERE SPORTS
Grasmere Sports Field. *Premier traditional Lakeland sports festival, featuring fell running, Cumberland wrestling, trade and craft stands, hound trials, etc.*
📞 015394 32127

HAWKSHEAD AGRICULTURAL SHOW
Hawkshead Hall Farm, Ambleside. *Major agricultural show, featuring trade and craft stands, traditional crafts, and farm animals.*
📞 015394 36553

LOWTHER HORSE-DRIVING TRIALS & COUNTRY FAIR
Lowther, Penrith. *Largest country sports event in Britain, featuring horse-driving trials.*
📞 01768 864190

SEPTEMBER
VICTORIAN FAIR
Kirkby Lonsdale. *Two-day festival featuring street entertainers, people dressed in period costume, etc.*
📞 Tourist Information Centre 015242 714 37

BORROWDALE SHEPHERDS' MEET & SHOW
Yew Tree Farm, Rasthwaite, Borrowdale. *Sheepdog trials and country show.*
📞 017687 77322

EGREMONT CRAB FAIR & SPORTS
Market Hall and Baybarrow Sports Field, Egremont. *Traditional regional events, including fell racing, wrestling, climbing a greasy pole, clay-pipe smoking and World Gurning Championship.*
📞 01946 821554

URSWICK RUSH-BEARING
Great and Little Urswick, near Ulverston. *Traditional procession through streets and church service.*
📞 01229 462768

OCTOBER
BUTTERMERE SHEPHERDS' MEETING & SHOW
Croft Farm, Buttermere. *Traditional Lakeland shepherds' meet and country show, featuring sheepdog and hound trials, sports and wrestling, singing and horn-blowing.*
📞 01900 821312

WASDALE HEAD SHOW & SHEPHERDS' MEET
Wasdale Head, Seascale. *Traditional shepherds' meet and show, with traditional sports and crafts.*
📞 019467 25340

WINDERMERE RECORD ATTEMPTS
Lowood Water Sports Centre, By Low Wood Hotel, Windermere. *World and national water sport record attempts.*
📞 015394 42595

DECEMBER
KIRKBY LONSDALE CHRISTMAS FAIR
Traditional switching on of Christmas lights by Father Christmas.
📞 Tourist Information Centre 015242 71437

REGIONAL SHOPPING

All of the larger towns, and most of the smaller ones, have an excellent selection of shops to suit all tastes, including the main high street chains. To make your stay in the Lake District just that little bit more memorable, however, we have selected a range of specialist shops that cater for the more discerning, with an eye for the unusual. Happy hunting!

ART & CRAFT SHOPS

Art & Craft shops are ever popular with visitors wishing to take home a special souvenir of their stay in Lakeland. Here are a few of our suggestions, several specialising in items made locally to make them just that little bit more individual.

APPLEBY
Courtland Gallery
Main Street
☎ 01768 351638
(Fine British crafts, pottery, glass, jewellery, original paintings.)

COCKERMOUTH
Pipkins
30 Market Place
☎ 01900 828867
(Local crafts.)

GRASMERE
Slapestones Galleries
Pye Lane
☎ 015394 35252
(Works by local artists.)

HAWES
Chapel Gallery
☎ 01969 667418
(Arts, crafts, gifts and pictures.)

KENDAL
The Barn Shop
Low Sizergh Farm
☎ 015395 60426
(Traditional arts and crafts.)

James Cropper
Burneside Mills
☎ 01539 722002
(Specialist paper-makers, gift sets.)

KIRKBY LONSDALE
The Loft Galleries
49 Main Street
☎ 015242 71833
(A unique museum-cum-gallery shopping experience.)

KIRKBY STEPHEN
Hartley Pine and Crafts
Unit 21 Hartley Fold
☎ 017683 72252
(Pine furniture and crafts.)

Heredities Ltd
Crossfield Mill
☎ 01768 371543
(Cold-cast figures made in bronze.)

MILLOM
Millom Craft Centre
Station Road
☎ 01229 770000
(Craft workshops, exhibition and gift shop.)

PENRITH
Wetheriggs Country Pottery
Clifton Dykes, near Penrith
☎ 01768 892733
(The only steam-powered pottery left in Britain. Watch potters at work and browse among an extensive range of items in the shop.)

WINDERMERE
Kentmere Studio Pottery
Staveley, near Windermere
☎ 01539 821621
(Hand-crafted traditional and gift ware.)

Made in Cumbria Craft Shop
Tourist Information Centre,
Victoria Street
☎ 015394 46499

GIFT SHOPS

The following is a small selection of gift shops offering exclusive items for those seeking something a little different, from ethnic jewellery and clothes to fine glass and china.

BERRIER
The Gem Den
Whitbarrow Hall, Whitbarrow Village
☎ 01768 483797
(Gems, precious stones and jewellery.)

BRAMPTON
Card Centre
44-46 Front Street
☎ 016977 2267
(Fancy goods, toys, jewellery, books and maps.)

Serendipity
12 Market Place
☎ 016977 41900
(Wood crafts and gift ideas.)

HAVERTHWAITE
Art Crystal
Clock Tower Buildings,
Low Wood
☎ 015395 31796
(Hand-engraved crystal ware.)

KENDAL
Kendal Foodhall
18-20 Finkle Street
☎ 01539 720323
(Take home some delicious Cumberland specialty foods as an unusual souvenir of your visit.)

The Mulberry Bush
19 Finkle Street
☎ 01539 730419
(Quality gifts and card shop.)

KIRKBY LONSDALE
The Sweet Shop
5 Market Square
☎ 015242 71570
(Home-made, traditional sweets!)

ULVERSTON
Colony Country Store
Lindal-in-Furness
☎ 01229 461102
(Watch traditional candle-making and choose from a selection of perfumed candles and accessories on sale.)

Cumbria Crystal
Lightburn Road
☎ 01229 584400
(Hand-made lead crystal in classic designs.)

Leather Mills
Gleaston Water Mill, Gleaston
☎ 01229 869077
(Leather goods, many gift ideas.)

Heron Glass
The Gill
☎ 01229 581121
(Unique range of glass art objects)

CLOTHING

The following shops specialise in outdoor leisure clothing (to enable you to enjoy your stay better) and also clothes made locally using traditional materials and manufacturing methods.

CARLISLE
The Mill Shop
Stead McAlpin, Cummersdale
☎ 01228 599589
(Selection of prints, weaves, dyed cottons and linens.)

KENDAL
K Village Factory Shopping
Lound Road
☎ 01539 732363

MORLAND
Travelling Light
Morland House, Morland,
Nr. Penrith
☎ 01931 714488
(Own unique range of travel, trekking and beach clothing.)

SEDBERGH
Farfield Clothing
The Old School
Joss Lane, Sedbergh
☎ 015396 20169
(Traditional outdoor clothing and factory shop.)

ULLSWATER
Alpaca Centre
Snuff Mill Lane, Stainton
(On A592, near Ullswater)
☎ 01768 891440
(Specialist shop offering a wide variety of Alpaca goods and clothes.)

ANTIQUES

There are many antique shops tucked away among the towns and villages of Lakeland, but visitors who are on a tighter time limit may find the establishment below of interest.

GB Antiques Centre
Lancaster Leisure Park,
Wyresdale Road, Lancaster
☎ 01524 844734
(More than 100 individual dealers offering all manner of antiques, collectors' items and curios at one of the largest antique centres in the country.)

MARKETS

Markets are always fun to explore and give the visitor a real flavour of the region. The following markets have been carefully selected for their overall interest value, offering a range of items from food, clothing and household goods, to gifts, souvenirs and specialist goods. For full details of location, etc, contact the relevant local Tourist Information Centre (see page 42).

Ambleside - Wed.
Appleby-in-Westmorland - Tues.
Barrow-in-Furness - Wed., Fri. & Sat.
Broughton-in-Furness - Tues.
Brampton - Wed.
Carlisle - Wed. & Sat.
Cockermouth - Mon.
Egremont - Fri.
Kendal - Wed. & Sat.
Keswick - Sat.
Lancaster Indoor Market - Daily
Maryport - Fri.
Morecambe covered market - Tues., Thur., Sat. & Sun.
Penrith - Tues.
Silloth - Fri.
Ulverston Market Hall - Mon., Tues., Thur., Fri. & Sat.
Ulverston Street Market - Thur. & Sat.
Whitehaven - Thur. & Sat.
Workington - Wed. & Sat.

SHOPPING CENTRES

Several towns in the Lake District have indoor shopping centres offering trouble-free shopping in any weather. The largest of these is the Westmorland Shopping Centre at Kendal.

General Information

The following information is provided to assist visitors in making their stay in the Lake District as trouble-free as possible. None of the lists claims to be exhaustive (space precludes us from listing all the available details), but this selection of the more important information should provide a useful starting point.

WINING AND DINING

The choice of eating establishments in the Lake District is limitless. Every town and most villages boast a range of pubs, cafés and restaurants, many specialising in delicious local recipes, and you are recommended to seek these out for yourself. Most places in the area cater very well for visitors, so the hungry or thirsty wayfarer is sure to find somewhere offering refreshments, from simple snacks and a cup of tea to full restaurant facilities. For that special occasion, however, the following list of restaurants have been singled out because of the excellence, and value, of their cuisine. There are many others, of course, and, again, we cannot recommend too strongly that you seek these out for yourself, but the following may prove to be a useful starting point.

AMBLESIDE

The Glass House
Rydal Road
☎ 015394 32137

The Kirkstone Galleries
Skelwith Bridge
☎ 015394 32553

Loughrigg Restaurant
Rothay Garth Hotel,
Rothay Road
☎ 015394 32217

Salutation Hotel
Lake Road
☎ 015394 32244

BARROW-IN-FURNESS

Abbey House Hotel
Abbey Road
☎ 01229 838282

Forum 28
Duke Street
☎ 01229 894758

Porthole Pantry
Dock Museum, North Road
☎ 01229 894231

BOWNESS-ON-WINDERMERE

Aunty Val's Tea Rooms
Church Street
☎ 015394 88211

Burn How Garden House Hotel,
Back Belsfield Road
☎ 015394 46226

English Lakes Hotel
Low Wood,
Windermere
☎ 015394 33773

Indian Cottage
Ash Street
☎ 015394 48544

BRAMPTON

The Howard Arms
Front Street
☎ 016977 2357

CARNFORTH

Morganna's
Pine Lake Resort
☎ 01524 738472

CARTMEL

Cavendish Arms Hotel
Cavendish at Cartmel
Cavendish Street
☎ 015395 36240

GREAT LANGDALE

Wainwright's Inn
The Langdale Estate
☎ 015394 38088

HAWKSHEAD

Highfield House
Country Hotel, Hawkshead Hill
☎ 015394 36344

Room With A View
The Square
☎ 015394 36751

KENDAL

J.R. Birketts
13 Market Place
☎ 01539 724206

Duffins Restaurant
54 Stramongate
☎ 01539 720387

Uptown Indian Restaurant
8 Stramongate
☎ 01539 723787

Waterside Wholefoods Vegetarian Café and Shop
Kent View
☎ 01539 729743

ORTON

New Village Tea Rooms
☎ 015396 24886

ULVERSTON

Armadale Country Restaurant
Arrad Foot
☎ 01229 861257

Chandler's Country Café
Lindal-in-Furness
☎ 01229 468322

Sting in the Tail
17 Fountain Street
☎ 01229 588028

WHERE TO DRINK

Britain, of course, is famed for the number and variety of its inns and pubs. Increasingly, more and more pubs offer a range of services and facilities, including accommodation, entertainment and meals to cover all tastes. Increasingly, more pubs now offer a range of real ales and fine wines. The following list of establishments is not intended to be definitive, but each is representative of the area in some way and may serve as a useful starting point. However the real joy of visiting pubs in this, region as in any other region of Britain, is in hunting out your own particular favourites - the list is endless.

KENDAL
The Ring O'Bells
Kirkland
☎ 01539 720326

KIRKBY LONSDALE
Snooty Fox Tavern
Main Street
☎ 015242 71308

PENRITH
The Dog and Gun Inn
Skelton
☎ 01768 484301

ULVERSTON
The Farmer's Arms
Market Place
☎ 01229 584469

BROUGHTON-IN-FURNESS
Blacksmith's Arms
Broughton Mills
☎ 01229 716824

GREAT ASBY
Three Greyhounds Inn
Near Appleby
☎ 017683 51428

The Shepherd's Inn
Melmerby
On the A686
☎ 01768 881217

Jenning's Brewery
Cockermouth
In addition to servicing many Lakeland pubs, Jenning's Brewery also holds brewery tours between May & October, providing an ideal opportunity to sample some of the local ale.
☎ 01900 823214

CARLISLE
Corby Bridge Inn
Off the A69, Great Corby
☎ 01228 560221

GREAT LANGDALE
Wainwright's Inn
The Langdale Estate
☎ 015394 38088

TUNSTALL
The Lunesdale Arms
Off the A683
☎ 015242 74203

NIGHTLIFE

The northwest region of Britain is generally quite well provided with theatres and concert halls, showing a wide range of entertainment including comedy, drama, opera, ballet, popular music and variety shows. There are also several cinemas showing the latest film releases. Obviously, such venues have a constantly changing programme, so booking office telephone numbers are provided here to enable you to check before-hand what might be showing.

BARROW-IN-FURNESS
Forum 28 Theatre and Arts Centre
28 Duke Street
☎ 01229 820000

CARNFORTH
Falcon's Lakeland Restaurant and Cabaret Bar
Pine Lake Resort
☎ 01524 736191

The Dome
Bubbles Leisure Park
Marine Road
(Leisure Centre & Theatre)
☎ 01524 831428

WORKINGTON
Carnegie Theatre and Arts Centre
Finkle Street
☎ 01900 602122

BOWNESS-ON-WINDERMERE
The Old Laundry Theatre
Crag Brow
☎ 015394 88444

KENDAL
The Brewery Arts Centre
Highgate
☎ 01539 725133

Superbowl
Central Drive
(Ten Pin Bowling)
☎ 01524 400974

Rosehill Theatre
Moresby
☎ 01946 692422

CARLISLE
Sands Centre
(Leisure Centre & Theatre)
☎ 01228 525222

KESWICK
Century Theatre
Lakeside
☎ 017687 74411

Frontierland
Morecambe Bay
☎ 01524 410024

And, of course, there is Blackpool, with its myriad of entertainment facilities on offer, from fun fairs, bingo halls, ballrooms and discos to theatres, cinemas and nightclubs, just a short distance away to the south of Lakeland.

Stanwix Arts Theatre
Brampton Road
☎ 01228 534664

MORECAMBE
Apollo 4 Cinema
Central Drive
☎ 01524 401040

WHITEHAVEN
Civic Hall
Lowther Street
☎ 01946 852821

GENERAL INFORMATION

TOURIST INFORMATION CENTRES

ALSTON
The Railway Station
☎ 01434 381696

AMBLESIDE
Market Cross
☎ 015394 32582

APPLEBY-IN-WESTMORLAND
Moot Hall,
Boroughgate
☎ 017683 51177

BARROW-IN-FURNESS
Forum 28, Duke Street
☎ 01229 870156

BOWNESS-ON-WINDERMERE
Glebe Road,
Bowness Bay
☎ 015394 42895

BRAMPTON
Moot Hall, Market Square
☎ 016977 3433

BROUGHTON-IN-FURNESS
Town Hall
☎ 01229 716115

CARLISLE
Old Town Hall
☎ 01228 625600

COCKERMOUTH
Town Hall
☎ 01900 822634

CONISTON
Ruskin Avenue
☎ 015394 41533

EGREMONT
Lowes Court Gallery,
12 Main Street
☎ 01946 820693

GRANGE-OVER-SANDS
Victoria Hall, Main Street
☎ 015395 34026

GRASMERE
Red Bank Road
☎ 015394 35245

HAWKSHEAD
Main Car Park
☎ 015394 36525

KENDAL
Town Hall,
Highgate
☎ 01539 725758

KESWICK
Moot Hall, Market Square
☎ 017687 72645

KILLINGTON LAKE
M6 Southbound
☎ 015396 20138

KIRKBY LONSDALE
Main Street
☎ 015242 71437

KIRKBY STEPHEN
Market Square
☎ 017683 71199

LONGTOWN
Memorial Hall,
Community Centre,
Arthuret Road
☎ 01228 791876

MARYPORT
Maritime Museum,
1 Senhouse Street
☎ 01900 813738

PENRITH
Museum, Robinson's School,
Middlegate
☎ 01768 867466

POOLEY BRIDGE
The Square
☎ 017684 86530

RAVENGLASS
Ravenglass and Eskdale
Railway Station
☎ 01229 717278

SEATOLLER THE BARN
☎ 017687 77294

SEDBERGH
72 Main Street
☎ 015396 20125

SELLAFIELD
Visitors' Centre
☎ 019467 76510

SILLOTH-ON-SOLWAY
The Green
☎ 01697 331944

SOUTHWAITE
M6 Service Area
☎ 016974 73445

ULLSWATER
Main Car Park,
Glenridding
☎ 017684 82414

ULVERSTON
Coronation Hall
☎ 01229 587120

WATERHEAD
Car Park
☎ 015394 32729

WHITEHAVEN
Market Hall, Market Place
☎ 01946 852939

WINDERMERE
Victoria Street
☎ 015394 46499

WORKINGTON
Central Car Park,
Washington Street
☎ 01900 602923

INFORMATION CENTRES

There are several places within the National Park where visitors can get information (in addition to the Tourist Information Centres, listed above) including:

Lake District National Park, Headquarters
Murley Moss,
Oxenholme Road, Kendal
☎ 01539 724555

BOWNESS-ON-WINDERMERE
Glebe Road, Bowness Bay
☎ 015394 42895

BROCKHOLE
On the main A591 road
between Windermere and Ambleside
☎ 015394 46601

CONISTON
Boating Centre
☎ 015394 41366

GRASMERE
Red Bank Road
☎ 015394 35245

GRIZEDALE FOREST
Visitor Centre
Hawkshead, Ambleside
☎ 015394 860010

HAWKSHEAD
Main Car Park
☎ 015394 36525

KESWICK
Moot Hall,
Market Square
☎ 017687 72645

POOLEY BRIDGE
The Square
☎ 017684 86530

SEATOLLER
Seatoller Barn
☎ 017687 77294

ULLSWATER
Main Car Park,
Glenridding
☎ 01768 482414

WATERHEAD
☎ 015394 32729

MORE INFORMATION

REGIONAL NEWSPAPERS

Local newspapers and periodicals which may be of interest to the visitor include: *North-West Evening Mail, News and Star, Cumbria and Lake District Magazine*, and *Lakeland Walker*. These are all widely available at newsagents and can be used to provide up-to-the-minute information.

LOCAL RADIO AND TELEVISION STATIONS

TELEVISION
The two local television stations for this region include B.B.C. North-West and Border Television.

RADIO
There are two local radio stations available, including B.B.C. Radio Cumbria (*756 AM* and *95.6 FM*) and CFM (*96.4, 103.4, 102.2* and *102.5 FM*).

USEFUL ADDRESSES

Cumbria Wildlife Trust
Brockhole,
Windermere
☎ 015394 48280

English Heritage
429 Oxford Street,
London (Headquarters)
☎ 0171 973 3434

English Nature
Juniper House,
Murley Moss, Kendal
☎ 01539 792800

Forestry Commission
Grizedale Forest Visitor Centre,
Hawkshead, Ambleside
☎ 015394 860010

**National Trust
for Cumbria**
The Hollens,
Grasmere, Ambleside
☎ 015394 35599

North-West Water
Chadwick House,
Warrington Road,
Risley, Warrington
☎ 01925 857000

SPORTING ACTIVITIES

In addition to the water sports, cycling and horse-riding activities already mentioned in the main text of this guide, the following sporting pastimes may also be of interest.

GOLF COURSES
Appleby Golf Club
Brackenber Moor
☎ 017683 51432

**Barrow-in-Furness
Golf Club**
Rakesmoor Lane, Hawcoat
☎ 01229 825444

Brampton Golf Course
Talkin Tarn
☎ 016977 2255

Carlisle Golf Club
Aglionby
☎ 01228 513303

Cockermouth Golf Club
Embleton
☎ 017687 76223

**Grange-over-Sands
Golf Club**
Meathop Road
☎ 015395 33180

Grange Fell Golf Club
Fell Road
☎ 015395 32536

Kendal Golf Club
The Heights
☎ 01539 724079

Keswick Golf Club
Threlkeld Hall
☎ 017687 79324

Maryport Golf Club
Bank End
☎ 01900 812605

Penrith Golf Club
Salkeld Road
☎ 01768 891919

Ulverston Golf Club
Bardsea
☎ 01229 582824

Windermere Golf Club
Cleabarrow
☎ 015394 43123

Workington Golf Club
Brainthwaite Road
☎ 01900 603460

ANGLING
Please make sure that you have the necessary licence and/or fishing permits before fishing in any of the rivers and lakes in the region. Ask for details at the nearest Tourist Information Centre. Permits are needed at the sites listed below.

Bassenthwaite Lake
Apply to Blencathra Centre, Threlkeld
(Coarse fishing)
☎ 017687 79633

Brampton
Apply to New Mills Trout Farm
(Fly fishing)
☎ 016977 2384

**Buttermere and
Crummock Water**
Apply to Ennerdale Farm
(Fly and coarse fishing)
☎ 017687 70232

Derwentwater
Apply to Field and Stream,
9 Main Street, Keswick
(Coarse fishing)
☎ 017687 74396

Loweswater
Apply to Water End Farm
(Coarse fishing)
☎ 01946 861465

WEATHER LINE

Because of the mountainous terrain, the weather in the Lake District can be very changeable. The mountains of Lakeland are often unforgiving in such circumstances. It is always a good idea to take the appropriate clothing to cover any eventuality if you intend being out for most of the day. It is also advisable to check the latest local weather forecast for an update before leaving, to make your trip as safe and enjoyable as possible.

Note that the weather on top of the fells is seldom the same as on the valley floors. What looks like a perfect, sunny day with blue skies from your hotel window can soon become a murky, misty day on the mountain summits - or vice versa! For more details, call the Lake District Weather Line.
☎ 017687 75757

ORDNANCE SURVEY MAPS

You are stongly advised to equip yourself with good maps if you intend venturing out into the fells. The rugged terrain can be surprisingly remote and many people become lost or disorientated if not properly equipped. Ordnance Survey publish an excellent series of four *Outdoor Leisure* maps (Sheets 4-7: *The English Lakes*) at a scale of 1:25,000 (2.5 inches to 1 mile/4 cm to 1 km). These maps are ideal for walkers because they show details such as contours, Public Rights of Way and Tourist Information. For a good overview of the area, refer to Sheet 5 (*Northern England*) in the Ordnance Survey *Routemaster* series.

General Information

ACCOMMODATION

Because of the rich diversity of accommodation available in Britain, ranging from simple camping and caravan sites and holiday camps to bed and breakfast establishments, guest houses and a wide range of hotels of all classes, it is generally assumed that individuals will want to book their accommodation themselves beforehand. Tourist Information Centres (see page 42) offer extensive lists of locally available accommodation and many operate a book-a-bed-ahead scheme for travellers.

HOW TO GET THERE

ROAD LINKS

Road access to the Lake District and the northwest region as a whole is excellent. The M6 motorway separates the Lake District from the Pennines and links the area to all of the major motorway networks of the North, the Midlands, London and the South.

Once off the motorways there is a good network of 'A' roads serving the Lake District, making all the main centres easily accessible. Some of the more remote areas are only accessible along country lanes and several of the mountain roads (which can be narrow and very steep) require special care, but generally, the network of roads within the region is excellent.

PARKING IN LAKELAND

The general rule when parking in Lakeland is to leave your car at a designated car park and walk to your destination. Do not expect to always be able to park exactly where you want. Also, do not park thoughtlessly or illegally on narrow roads so as to cause a nuisance or an obstruction.

Most people come to the Lakes because they want to escape the pressures of urban life and are more than happy to walk a few extra yards. With this in mind, some of the locations described in this guide are a little way from a convenient car park. Always allow a little extra time for an additional walk to and from your car where necessary.

At best, cars spoil the view (and the photographs!); at worst, careless parking can be positively dangerous. Details of parking permits and the availability of car parks in the Lake District can be acquired from the Tourist Information Centres listed on page 42.

RAIL LINKS

There is good rail access to the perimeters of Lakeland, but virtually none in the interior. From Carnforth, just north of Morecambe, a main line goes west to link up all of the coastal towns between there and Carlisle. A short branch line runs from Oxenholme to Kendal and Windermere, but goes no further into the mountains of Lakeland.

Until recently, all of Britain's rail network came under the auspices of the nationalised British Rail, but this has now been broken up into several individual private companies. It is not always necessary to break long journeys when crossing between regions, but each company has a slightly different operating procedure. If in doubt, check at local stations. There is a direct rail link from London, Euston, to Penrith and Carlisle. For Kendal and Windermere change at Oxenholme, while for the west coast line change at Lancaster. A fast network of Inter-City trains also connects several towns in the region to all other regions of Britain.

National Rail Enquiries
☏ 0345 484950

Rail Ticket Sales
☏ 0345 125625

AIRPORTS

The Lake District is not served directly by an airport. The nearest regional airports (which are also international airports) are Newcastle-upon-Tyne and Manchester, from where connecting coach and train services are available.

PUBLIC TRANSPORT

Public transport in the Lake District is good locally, but most services operate within a limited catchment area and several operate during the summer months only. For local timetable information contact the relevant Tourist Information Centre in the first instance. They will be able to give you the contact number for local bus operatives. Also, Cumbria County Council employs a public transport team who work with all bus, coach, train and ferry operators in an effort to advise on the best transport available for both visitors and residents. For information, contact:

Journey Planner Service
☏ 01228 606000

The Cumbria Journey Planner public transport information system is also now available on the Internet at the following site:
http://www.cumbria.gov.uk.

For general enquiries regarding public transport, telephone the following enquiry help line:

Cumbria County Council
☏ 01228 812812

COACH OPERATORS

Britain has several extensive networks of privately-run coach companies that provide regular services to the main towns of the Lake District and to all other regions. The following companies operate within the area:

National Express Coach Services
☏ 0990 808080

Stagecoach Cumberland
☏ 01946 63222

EXCURSIONS

Several coach companies also run excursions to places of interest throughout the region. Check with your hotel, or contact the nearest Tourist Information Centre for details. There are also excursions to some of the more remote locations in the Lake District. Contact:

Mountain Goat Mini Coach Tours
☏ 015394 45161

FERRIES

There are several ferry services operating on the Lakes, which can be used for leisure or as part of your overall journey plan to eliminate certain sections of road travel. Some of the services are only available during the summer months, however, and you are advised to check details with the appopriate local Tourist Information Centre. Details of sailing times are also given on the Cumbria Journey Planner (see 'Public Transport' above).

CAR RENTAL

All of the major car rental companies operate in the Lake District, but there are many local companies too, offering competitive rates. Our advice is to shop around.

ACCESS FOR THE DISABLED

The very nature of the landscape in Lakeland can

make life difficult for the disabled. Where possible, those locations that offer special facilities for their needs have been selected. Unfortunately, however, a number of the scenic delights of the region are only accessible to able-bodied people on foot, by walking the fells.

OVERSEAS VISITORS

DRIVING

Always ensure that you have the necessary driving permits and insurance before driving in the U.K. Drive on the left side of the road, and at roundabouts, give way to the right, unless otherwise instructed. Signposting is generally very good, but you should purchase a copy of the Highway Code for clarification. Road surfaces are generally excellent. Use designated car parks whenever possible and never park on double yellow lines on the road edge.

HEALTH CARE

Before travelling to the U.K. you should ensure that you have been suitably inoculated (according to your country of origin). There are no prevalent infectious diseases in the U.K. and no vaccinations are required. The water is safe to drink straight from the tap. Whilst here, you will be entitled to free health care at National Health Service hospitals, although some, or all, of the cost may be recharged to you if your country of origin does not have a reciprocal arrangement with the U.K. Please note that dental and eye care is not free.

VAT REFUNDS

Overseas visitors can apply for a refund of VAT for purchases over £50. Ask for a form when making your purchase.

ELECTRICITY

The electricity supply in Britain uses 240 volts AC. Plug adapters are available in most electrical appliance stores.

TIPPING

There is no formal system for tipping in Britain, and it still remains a highly debatable issue. Generally, a tip of about 10% is acceptable at restaurants, hairdressers and for taxi drivers. Hotel porters might expect a £1 coin tip. Elsewhere, tipping is not generally expected, though, of course, this is up to the individual. Some restaurants have taken to including a tip (called a service charge) in with the bill.

WALKING & CYCLING

GETTING OUT & ABOUT

One of the finest ways to explore any region is to use the Public Rights of Way that criss-cross every part of this country. Britain possesses a unique network of some 120,000 miles (193,080 km) of public footpaths, bridleways and byways, most crossing private land. This network of paths was not created in recent ages for recreational purposes, but is rooted firmly in history, some perhaps being as much as 4,000 years old. They formed part of the highways network in the past, used by villagers to get to work or church, or by traders carrying their wares. They are still maintained as highways by local authorities and are protected in law. Often located in beautiful, remote countryside, there is no better way to see Britain.

TYPES OF PATH

There are three main types of Public Rights of Way:

Footpaths
For use on foot only.

Bridleways
For use on foot, horseback or bicycle.

Byways
For use on foot, horseback, bicycle or in any other vehicle. Most are unmade surfaces and are waymarked by yellow, blue and red arrows respectively.

Please note:
Cyclists should never use footpaths. They are only legally entitled to use bridleways, byways or other carriageways.

KNOW YOUR RIGHTS

Although the Local Highways Authority is responsible for maintaining Public Rights of Way, it rarely owns the land over which the paths run. Landowners, therefore, can claim a greater right of use and are permitted to plough cross-field paths, provided they are reinstated within two weeks, though headland paths should never be ploughed. It is illegal to obstruct a path or otherwise prevent someone from using it and all irregularities should be reported to the Local Highways Authority. Paths can be legally diverted or stopped-up, however, though notices must be posted and new routes waymarked.

A copy of all Public Rights of Way is maintained by the relevant Highways Authority and can usually be consulted at any reasonable time. The routes shown in this guide were accurate at the time of going to press, but things can change. If you are in any doubt about your rights, or the routes, contact the relevant Highways Authority at:

Cumbria County Council
📞 01228 606060

General Information

When using the Public Rights of Way network, please always show care and consideration for landowners and people living in the locality (especially when parking) and follow the Country Code at all times.

WHAT TO TAKE

The pull-out walks and cycle rides in this guide have been specially selected so that they are suitable even for the inexperienced. It is usually best to travel as light as possible, but always wear appropriate footwear and clothing. Although those places selected here have at least some facilities, it is generally best to assume that none will be available. You should plan your itinerary accordingly and take essential supplies and refreshments with you in case, for any reason, they are not available on the route.

Remember to tell someone where you are planning to go, in case of an accident. Although some may prefer the solace of lone walking or cycling, it is usually better to take at least one companion (or a mobile phone) in case of emergency. You should always take the relevant O.S. *Pathfinder* or *Explorer* map.

ADDITIONAL INFORMATION FOR SAFE CYCLING

Always ensure that your bicycle is in good working order and that it is the correct size. Take great care on the roads, especially with right turns; if necessary, dismount and cross the road on foot. When out riding it is essential to wear bright clothing, carry lights and take waterproofs. Always carry refreshments, a small tool kit, puncture repair kit, first-aid kit and enough money for emergencies. It is important to stay alert at all times; be ready for pedestrians on narrow lanes and fast traffic on main roads. Finally, always follow the advice contained in the Highway Code.

THE COUNTRY CODE

- *Enjoy the countryside and respect its life and work.*
- *Guard against all risk of fire.*
- *Leave all gates as you find them.*
- *Keep all dogs under close control.*
- *Keep to public paths across farmland.*
- *Use gates and stiles to cross fences, hedges and walls.*
- *Leave livestock, crops and machinery alone.*
- *Take your litter home.*
- *Help to keep all water clean.*
- *Protect wildlife, plants and trees.*
- *Take special care on country roads.*
- *Make no unnecessary noise.*

WHEN THINGS GO WRONG

IF YOU ARE UNWELL

For routine accidents or health problems contact the local hospital of the region you are staying in. Local doctors will also usually see visitors - contact your nearest Tourist Information Centre for details (see page 42) or ask at your hotel or a chemist shop. General information on N.H.S services and treatments is available from:

National Health Service
☎ 0800 665544

EMERGENCIES

In the case of genuine emergencies *only* dial 999, free of charge. Speak slowly and clearly and give the operator details of which service you require: Ambulance, Police, Fire Brigade, Mountain Rescue, Cave Rescue or Coastguard. (NB: An alternative emergency telephone number to use is 112.)

LIFEGUARDS

Several local authorities now provide Lifeguard services at beaches within their control. If you see someone in difficulty in the water, always contact the lifeguard where possible rather than attempt a rescue yourself.

POLICE

For all non-urgent police matters, you should contact:

Cumbria Constabulary Force
☎ 01768 891999

MOUNTAIN RESCUE

Despite the warnings, every year a small number of people get into difficulties on the mountains, sometimes as the result of an accident, but more often as the result of not being suitably equipped for the particular activity being undertaken. If you get into difficulties, or see someone else in trouble, call the emergency services (see above) and give as clear directions as possible to the location of the injured person.

Most problems can be averted by being properly prepared before venturing out and treating the mountains with respect. Do not be misled into thinking that their relatively low stature means that they can be treated lightly. The northerly latitude of Britain gives our mountains a severity often associated with peaks much higher.

MONEY MATTERS

The list of banks and building societies throughout the Lake District would be too lengthy to include here. Most of the larger towns throughout the region will have branches of these institutions, including the four main banks (Barclays, Midland, National Westminster and Lloyds). Tourist Information Centres will be able to give you a complete list of branches of all banks or building societies.

BUREAU DE CHANGE

Most main branches of banks and building societies also operate a foreign money exchange service. Check with individual branches for details. Travellers' cheques and Eurocheques are also widely accepted at shops and restaurants.

CREDIT CARDS

All major credit and debit cards are accepted throughout Britain, including Visa, Mastercard, American Express, Diners, Switch and Delta.

INDEX

A
Abbot Hall Art Gallery 31
Abbots Reading Farm 8
Alavna 31
Allonby Bay 4
Ambleside 12, 22
animals 7, 8, 9, 25
Appleby Castle 26
Aquarium of the Lakes 10
Armboth 33
Ashness Bridge 19

B
balloon trips 15
Barrow-in-Furness 24, 30
The Beacon, Whitehaven 6
Berwick-on-Tweed 2
Birdoswald 25
Birthwaite see Windermere
Blackpool Pleasure Beach 9
Blea Tarn 18
border disputes 2, 25
Border Regiment Museum 25
Bowness-on-Windermere 8, 13, 15, 30, 35
Bragg, Melvyn 3
Brantwood 23, 28
Brathay, River 18, 19
Brockhole Visitors' Centre 11
Brough Castle 26
Brougham Castle & Hall 26

C
Campbell, Donald 8
Cark-in-Cartmel 8, 29
Carlisle 2, 25, 31, 34
'Cars of the Stars' Motor Museum 10
Cartmel 21
Castlerigg Stone Circle 27
Cat Bells 18
Christian, Fletcher 6
Cistercian Way 24
Clifford family 26
climbing 14
Cockermouth 22
Coleridge, S.T. 3, 22
Coniston 12, 23, 28
Crossgates 7
Cumberland Pencil Museum 10
Cumbria Crystal 11
Cumbria Cycle Way 15
cycling 15, cards

D
Dalton Leisure Centre 9
Derwentwater 19, 32
Derwentwater Marina 14
Dock Museum 30
Dove Cottage 13, 22

E
Elterwater 18
emergencies 46
entertainment 41
events 36-7

F
Fairfield Horseshoe ridge walk 20
farming 3, 8
Fell Foot Park 17
ferry services 12, 13, 16, 17
Forest Enterprise 7
Friar's Crag 32
Furness Abbey 24
Furness Railway 7

G
geology 2, 3, 31, 32
Gleaston Water Mill 25
Grange-over-Sands 5
Grasmere 13, 22
Great Gable 32
Great Langdale 19, 33
Great Langdale Beck 18
Greenburn 19
Greta Hall 22
Grizedale Visitor Centre 7

H
Hadrian's Wall 25
Hardknott Pass & Roman fort 16
Harris Museum & Art Gallery 30
Haverthwaite 7, 8, 17
Hawkshead 34
Helvellyn 33
High Sweden Bridge 20
Hill Top, Sawrey 11, 23
Hoghton Tower 27
Holker Hall & Gardens 8, 29
Hutton-in-the-Forest 24

I
information 42-6
Inglewood family 24
Ismay, T.H. 6

K
Kendal 23, 28, 31
Kent, River 31
Keswick 10, 22, 27
Kirkstone Pass 20, 32

L
lake cruises 16
Lake District National Park 2, 11, 21
Lakeland Motor Museum 8, 29
Lakeland Wildlife Oasis 9
Lakeside & Haverthwaite Railway 7, 8, 17
Lancaster 27, 35
Langdale Pikes 18, 33
Laurel & Hardy Museum 9
Levens Hall & Gardens 28
Little Langdale 18, 19
Loweswater 21
Lowther family 4
Lowther Leisure Park 6
Lune, River 35
Lunecastrum 35

M
maritime history 6, 30
Marshall, William 21
Maryport 6, 31
Milnthorpe 9
mining 12, 17
Morecambe 5
Morecambe Bay 5, 24
mountain biking 15
mountain climbing 14
'Mountain Goat' mini coach tours 16
Muncaster Castle, Gardens & Owl Centre 29
Museum of Lakeland Life & Industry 31
museums 6-11, 30-1

N
Naval Reserve Battery 31
Newby Bridge 10, 17
Normans 25, 26, 27

INDEX & ACKNOWLEDGMENTS

O
Owl Centre 29

P
Pattinson, George 30
Pele towers 24, 26, 28
Penrith 24, 26
pony trekking 15
Pooley Bridge 12
Portinscale 14
Potter, Beatrix 3, 7, 8, 11, 23
Preston 30

R
railways 7, 17, 35
Ratty Arms 17
Ravenglass 29
Ravenglass & Eskdale Railway 17
Romans 16, 25, 26, 27, 31, 35
Ruskin, John 3, 23, 28

Rydal Mount 13, 22, 29
Rydal valley 20

S
St. Bees 4
St. John's Beck 21
Sawrey 11, 23
Scafell 2, 32
Scandale Beck 20
Sellafield Visitor Centre 17
Senhouse Roman Museum 31
shopping 38-9
Silloth 5
Sizergh Castle & Gardens 29
Skelwith Bridge 18
Skelwith Force 19
Skiddaw 2, 19, 32
Slater's Bridge 19
South Lakes Wild Animal Park 7
Steamboat Museum 30

Stock Ghyll Force 20
Strickland family 28
Striding Edge 33
'The Struggle' 20
'Swallows & Amazons' 30

T
Thirlmere 21, 33
Tullie House Museum & Art Gallery 31

U
Ullswater 32
Ulverston 9, 11, 25

V
Vale of St. John 21

W
Wainwright, Alfred 3, 23
walking 6, 7, 17, 19, 20, 33, 45,
Wasdale valley 32

Wast Water 32
water sports 4, 5, 14
waterfalls 19, 20
Waterhead 33
Whitehaven 4, 6
Whittington 36
Windermere 13, 33, 35
Windermere Lake Cruises 7, 13
wining & dining 40-1
Wordsworth, Dorothy 22
Wordsworth, William 3, 13, 22, 29, 32, 34
Wordsworth House 22
World of Beatrix Potter 7, 8
World Owl Trust 29
Wythburn 33

Z
zoos 7, 9

ACKNOWLEDGEMENTS

We would like to thank: John Guy, Elaine Wilkinson, David Hobbs, Elizabeth Wiggans, Nicola Godfrey-Evans, Geoffrey Cook, Lake District National Park Authority and The Cumbria Tourist Board for their assistance.
Copyright © 1999 ticktock Publishing Ltd.
First published in Great Britain by ticktock Publishing Ltd., The Offices in the Square, Hadlow, Tonbridge, Kent TN11 0DD, Great Britain. All rights reserved.
No part of this publication may be reproduced, stored in a retrieval system, or transmitted in any form or by any means, electronic, mechanical, photocopying, recording or otherwise, without prior written permission of the copyright owner.

A CIP catalogue record for this book is available from the British Library. ISBN 1 86007 134 1
Picture research by Image Select. Printed in Hong Kong.

Picture Credits: t=top, b=bottom, c=centre, l=left, r=right

Graham Kirk; OFC. Greg Evans; 40bl, 46cb. Image Select; 2tl, 14t. J. Allan Cash; IFC (main pic), 4br, 5tl, 5cr, 5br, 16cr, 21b, 41cl, 43t, 45c. Pictor; OFC (main pic). Spectrum Colour Library; OFC, 4cl, 8l, 13t, 13bl, 13cr, 15b, 25bl, 28br, 35l, 38tl, 39tr, 46cl, cycle card 2.
Some of the additional images were supplied digitally by Corel Ltd. The pull-out walks and cycle routes were kindly verified by Cumbria County Council Highways Department and the Lake District National Park Authority.

Every effort has been made to ensure that the information in this book is as up-to-date as possible at the time of going to press. However, details such as telephone numbers, opening hours, prices and travel information are liable to change. The publishers cannot accept responsibility for any consequence arising from the use of this book.
Please send any corrections and suggestions for improvement in the next edition to: HMTE ticktock Publishing, The Offices in the Square, Hadlow, Tonbridge, Kent TN11 0DD.

ticktock
publishing ltd